An Old River Town

Being a History of Winterport, (Old Frankfort), Maine, Illustrated From Photographs

By Ada Douglas Littlefield

PANTIANOS
CLASSICS

Published by Pantianos Classics

ISBN-13: 978-1-78987-537-9

First published in 1907

The Village Today (1907)

Contents

"Often I think of that beautiful town

   That is seated by the sea.

Often in thought go up and down

The pleasant streets of that dear old town

   And my youth comes back to me."

Longfellow.

To Any Reader

In this book I have attempted to give sketches taken round about the town of Winterport, Maine, formerly a part of "old Frankfort." It is not a history in the ordinary acceptation of the term. The early town records were destroyed by fire so that it has been necessary to collect facts of local history from records of surrounding towns, old letters, diaries, court records and numerous other sources. Many anecdotes have been told me; but all historical facts I have tried to verify. At the end of the book is a list of authorities consulted in its preparation.

My thanks are due to all those, too numerous to mention, who have made the book, for the pleasant hours spent in happy reminiscence when only the best and brightest side of people was pictured.

I am specially indebted to Mrs. Frank Haley for the use of the Goodwin diary which covered a period of many years, for old letters, account books and many articles of historic interest; to Mrs. Harriet Newell Abbott, for valuable information, for the loan of old papers and copies of records, also for the use of photographs and furniture; to Mrs. Mary Haley, for the use of old papers, books, letters and deeds, and for access to articles of wearing apparel, dishes and furniture; to Mr. Frank Kelly, for records, letters and charts; to Mr. E. P. Treat of Frankfort, for information about shipbuilding, for the use of manuscript and the chart of Penobscot River. Most of the photographs were taken by Miss Helen Louise Eveleth.

The sons and daughters of Maine return now and again from every part of the Union to the Pine Tree State; and among them come "old residents" of Winterport, returning to their homes on the Penobscot. They look for some familiar face and are told "Look on the hill," or "He's buried up yonder," and their calls are made as often at the cemetery as at the old homesteads. To these scattered sons and daughters, and to those at home, this book is dedicated.

Possibly the present citizens — those who have taken the fathers' places — may find in it an inspiration to greater achievement because of those who have lived before them. The children now, the future fathers and mothers, may see that there is self-denial and generosity for them to emulate.

A woman once said to me: "I tell you there is no man here, in this generation, who can come up to those men of old for intelligence and public spirit." She was wrong indeed. The descendants of these "men of old" can and do come up to their fathers in intelligence and public spirit. They are right here in town, and others are standing first in other places as doctors, lawyers, public benefactors, sea captains and business men.

We of the younger generation accept the town as it was left us — with its buildings, its churches, its libraries, our homes, the streets and trees. We accept them, little realizing what they cost in thought, labor, money and self-denial; and our appreciation is too small for what they merit.

If any of the accounts given should attract strangers who would offer gold for our treasures, may it be refused; one and all they should be kept here and cherished for the sake of early memories and the days of "auld lang syne."

Ada Douglas Littlefield.

Winterport, Maine,
November First, 1907.

An Old River Town

I - The Country

The town of Winterport lies on the west bank of the Penobscot river —
latitude 44:38 and longitude 68:50. It is a part of the old town of Frankfort
and was incorporated as a separate town in April, 1860, just before the Civil
War; and — if stories are true — just after a warm local war, the details of
which are better forgotten. In name we were the losers; for as one has remarked, "Frankfort seems to carry with it much more dignity," which is true.
However there is but one Winterport in the United States or in the world, for
that matter; and it is said that a letter directed here without the state address
will reach its destination safely.

The town covers thirty-six and one-half square miles and quite a history
might be made if one told the story of all the grants, titles, and rulers which
the land has been under.

The country was first called Acadia and came under French rule in 1603
when De Mong took possession. In 1605 Weymouth planted the cross in the
name of James I, of England. Then Captain John Smith explored the northeastern coast in 1614 and gave to it the name New England. Under the pro-
vincial charter made in 1639, this land was included in the Province of
Maine. In 1643 Massachusetts Bay included all the settlements of Maine and
New Hampshire. Afterwards the Commonwealth of Massachusetts took possession of Maine.

When in 1773 the one hundred thousand acres belonging first to the Ten
Proprietors and afterward to General Waldo were set off, what is now Win-
terport was included with Frankfort, Hampden, and parts of Swanville, Mon-
roe, and Bangor. The grant had been known in turn by the names Muscongus,
Lincolnshire, and Waldo patent. The patent for the land bears the date "ye
Thirteenth day of March in ye first year of ye Reign of our Soveraign Lord
Charles," 1629.

General Waldo did much for the development of the Penobscot valley.
Through his influence Fort Pownall was built and he was back of the governor in his efforts. During a visit to his estate at this time, his untimely death
occurred and his burial took place at Fort Point. No monument marked his
resting place but his name lives in two towns, a county, and the mountain at
Marsh Bay. The historian Drake says that his remains were removed to Boston.

Forty thousand acres of his estate came into the hands of General Knox.
The early years of this General were brilliant. It was at the siege of Boston

that he first came to the attention of Washington. He was then given important offices. He took part in the battles of Trenton, Princeton, Brandywine, Germantown, Monmouth, and Yorktown; and finally superintended the disbanding of the Continental Army. He built a fine residence at Thomaston hoping to spend his last years there; but extravagant living forced him to mortgage the property, and finally it was sold through Sears, Thorndike, and Prescott. Mr. Albert Kelly of this town was agent for them.

A deed dated 1753 speaks of land "in the district called Frankfort on the east side of Kennebeck River in the county of York"; and one in 1772 mentions "a new plantation called Frankfort." It was voted in the House of Representatives in 1755 that ninety men be employed for scouting, "from New Boston to Frankford, and one hundred men from Frankford to the Truck House on St. George's river." The plantation name of Pownalboro, the fifteenth incorporated town, was Frankfort. Then, in 1754, near Dresden, a fortress was erected called Frankfort, afterward renamed Fort Shirley.

Thus Frankfort seems to have been a favorite name. This may be accounted for by the fact that throughout Maine were many French forts and the old name, Frank, was substituted for French, the name thus becoming Frankfort. The derivation of Frankford may be accounted for in the same way.

The story of the incorporation of the town may be read in the following petitions and acts: —

"The Hon. Senate and House of Representatives in General Court Assembled.

"The Petition and Memorial of the Subscribers Inhabitants of the Plantation of Frankfort in the County of Lincoln bounded as follows, Vizt. Beginning at the South-eastwardmost corner of Belfast on ye sea (or Bay) shore from thence running in the line of s'd Belfast, to the Northeastwardmost Ejctremity thereof, from thence North to a Large Spruce tree on the eastwardly side of Goose pond (so called) Marked with a Marking Iron W. P. B. F. two large white stones on the westwardly side of said pond. Directly in range and bearing due north from s'd tree; From thence eastwardly to Marsh river so called; From thence Down said Marsh river, about a mile to Penobscot river; From thence down said Penobscot river Southwardly to Fort Point so called; From said fort point westwardly to the first mentioned bounds at Belfast.

"Humbly Sheweth there are now living upon said plantation upwards of Sixty Families who Labour under great disadvantages for want of being Incorporated with Town privileges; Therefore Humbly pray your Honors to take into your wise Consideration our Present very disagreeable situation and relieve us by Incorporating us, together with the adjacent Island of Brigadiers Island so called into a town by the name of Knoxbury.

"Your Petitioners as in Duty bound will ever Pray:
"Frankfort,
"May ye 16, 1789."

John Odam,	Ichabod Colson,	William Dickey,
James Nichols,	Ebenezer Griffing,	John Peirce,
Benj. Shute,	Daniel Goodell,	Joshua Treat,
David Nichols,	Longworthy	Dan Lancaster,
Henry Black,	Lampher,	John Odam, Jr.,
James Nichols, Jr.,	Jacob Eustis,	John Staples,
Jas. Crary,	Miles Staples,	John Sweetzer,
Barah Ellis,	William Pendleton,	David Partridge,
Alexander Young,	William Staples,	James Grant,
Peleg Pendleton,	Samuel Griffing,	Benj. Shute, Jr.,
Samuel Young,	Jotham Staples,	Joseph McMann.
John Park,	Samuel Griffing, Jr.,	Clark Partridge,
William Griffing,	Thos. Fletcher,	
Zethan French,	William Hitchborn,	

The "Gen'l Court" took prompt action on this petition and June 25, 1789, passed an act incorporating a town by the name of Frankfort, in the same year that Washington was elected and inaugurated as first president. It embraced all of the present towns of Frankfort, Winterport, Prospect, Stockton Springs, Searsport, and parts of Hampden and Newburgh, which made a very large town. The following is a copy of the Act of Incorporation:

"Commonwealth of Massachusetts.

In the year of our Lord, one thousand seven hundred and eighty-nine.

"An Act to incorporate the plantation from Belfast to Wheeler's Mills, West side of Penobscot River in the County of Lincoln, into a Town by the name of Frankfort.

"Be it enacted by the Senate and House of Representatives in General Court assembled, and by the Authority of the same; That the Tracts of Land bounded as followeth, viz.. Northeasterly on the Bay of Belfast, and Penobscot River up said river to Wheeler's Mills. Thence by a line beginning at the Southeast corner of Belfast and running due North, on the eastern bounds of Belfast, until a line running due West from said Wheeler's Mills shall intersect the same, together with the Inhabitants thereon, be and are hereby. Incorporated into a Town, by the Name of Frankfort, and the inhabitants of the said Town are hereby invested with all the powers, privileges, and immunities which the inhabitants of Towns within this Commonwealth do or may by law enjoy.

"Also be further enacted that Benjamin Shute, Esq., is hereby authorized and empowered to issue his Warrant directed to some suitable Inhabitant of the said town of Frankfort, directing him to notify the Inhabitants of the said Town, to meet at such time and place as he shall appoint, to choose such officers, as other Towns are empowered to choose at their Annual Meetings in the Months of March or April Annually.

"In the

"This Bill having had three several readings, passed to be engrossed.

"Sent up for concurrence.

"David Cobb, Sp'kr.

"In Senate June 24, 1787, this Bill having had two several readings, passed a concurrence to be engrossed.

"Saml. Phillips, Jr., Presedt."

However the petitioners were not satisfied with the act. The town was too large, the name was opposed; and again they petitioned the General Court. Here follows the second petition, and the plan annexed was drawn by Joseph P. Martin.

"The Honorable Senate, and House of Representatives in General Court assembled —

"The Petition and Memorial of the Subscribers, Inhabitants of the Plantation of Frankfort in the County of Hancock.

"Humbly sheweth

That whereas, the Honorable General Court, did by an act passed ye 25th of June 1789, incorporating two Plantations of the west side of Penobscot River, viz. from Belfast to Wheeler's Mills: into a town, by the name of Frankfort: which for want of a true representation of our boundaries being seasonably exhibited we presume that an undesigned mistake has been made: as the two plantations are about sixteen miles in length, and very inconvenient for one town. — There are now upwards of sixty families in this Plantation.

"We therefore, humbly pray your Honors to take into your wise consideration, our Present difficult situation: and incorporate us, together with the adjacent Island, called Brigadiers Island, (separate from the other Plantation) according to the following boundaries and plan annexed — viz.: beginning at the southeast corner of Belfast, running up the brook, to ye northeast corner of said Belfast: thence north to goose pond, thence along the shore of said pond, to a large spruce tree, on the east side of goose pond, marked with a marking Iron W. P. B. F.: thence eastwardly to Marsh River: thence east down s'd Marsh River to Penobscot River: thence down Penobscot River to Fort Point, thence bounding on the bay of Penobscot, to the bounds first mentioned, into a town by the name of Knoxburgh.

"Your Petitioners as in duty bound, will pray;

"Frankfort Plantation, Nov. 28, 1789.

Daniel Lancaster,	John Cleford,	Wm. Pendleton,
John Dwelly,	John Odam Jur,	Isaac Clewley,
John Sweetser,	Jacob Cleford,	John Sweetser, Jr.,
Josh'a Treat,	John Odam,	Samuel Young,
Daniel Goodele, Jr.,	Alex'r Young,	William Dickey,
Abraham Mudgett,	Peleg Pendleton,	Nath'l Tebbets
Henry Black,	David Patridge,	Nathaniel Cleford,

Benjamin Shute, Junr.,
Joseph G. Martin,
Joseph Boyd,
Zethan French,
Samuel Grant,
William Farley,
James Scott,
David Nichols,
Henry Lord,
John Staples,

Miles Staples,
James Grant,
Joseph McMann,
Samuel Griffin,
John Park,
Henry Black, Jur.,
Josiah Ames,
Jacob Eustis,
Daniel Goodell,
Ebenezer Griffin,

Longworthy Lampher,
James Nichols,
James Nichols, 2nd,
John Peirce,
Thomas McMann,
William Staples,
Clark Partridge,
William Hichborn,
Wm. McLaughlin,

"In the House of Representatives January 13, 1790.

"Read and committed to the Standing Committee on applications for Incorporations of Towns to consider and report.

"Sent up for concurrance.

"David Cobb, Spkr.

"In Senate Feb'yl. 1790.

"Read and concurred,

"Tho. Dawes, Presedt., Pro Tem."

It is not known just why the name Knoxburg or Knoxbury was not given, for both were in honor of General Knox, the trusted friend of Washington. General Knox and Governor Hancock were not friends however and the latter may have used some influence in the matter.

The records report no further action taken on the last petition. The first act of incorporation was never changed and the name Frankfort was retained. Among various conjectures as to the origin of the name, one has been that it was named for Frankfort-on-the-Main in Germany.

The first survey of the town was known as the Chadwick Survey and was made in 1772. A line was run from the Cove straight to the Marsh Stream at a point near the spring. (This spring lies just beyond the Guide Board.) The line extended one mile back from and parallel with the river. Every twenty rods along the line, granite posts were set up, dividing it into one-hundred-acre lots. From the top of Cobb's Mountain at Bucksport Center the boundary of meuiy of these lots may still be seen, marked clearly by bushes or trees which have grown up along the old stone fences. This is known as the "Chadwick line." The plan of the survey showed houses at the following points: one each on the Sampson and McGlathry lots where were the two earliest log houses; one on the Low's Brook lot occupied by Low; one on the Dunton lot occupied by Samuel Wilson; and one on the lot occupied by Hatevil Colson.

We read of many other settlers who came at about this time: William Sullivan, who came from Georgetown in 1774; and Ichabod Colson, who had been at Fort Pownall, also settled here. In 1787 "Tobias Oakman of Boston, yeoman" bought land. The next year Reuben Goodwin, from a "place called Marsh Bay," was selling land. In 1789 John Bowlin, a shipwright, and Miller

11

Johnston were here. The Kemptons, John and Zacheus, were at Oak Point. We read also of James Colson; and Moses Littlefield, a Revolutionary hero. This same year Francis LeBaron Goodwin came from Plymouth and his diary gives this account of his journey hither.

"1789 Apr. 14 Sett off with John Kempton for the Eastward to look up a Farm to live on. Arrived at Penobscot at Wm. Colsons of whom I purchased fifty acres of land with an Intent to live there. We lived on Oak point until ye 1st of June and then went to Fox Islands to Load in Boards. Capt. Bartlet and Holmes came down to us and the next day we set off for Plymouth — arrived here ye 12 of June." Oak Point must have received its name before this date.

A second survey was begun in 1808 and the field notes are under this title.

"Description of the lots on the Ten Proprietors' Patent
  which includes the Town of Frankfort in the County of Hancock.
  Containing in the whole 43,132 acres.
                    Surveyed by
                                          Seth Herrick Surv.
Commenced July 26, 1808 and completed March 9th, 1816. with Plans."
The following letter tells something of the country Mr. Herrick found.

"To Messrs Thorndike Sears & Prescott as many parts of this Patent are very rough surveying and the lots in every part have been taken up by the settlers in irregular and in some instances intricate form, much labor and care have been necessary to obtain an exact account of their form and contents. The timber of many descriptions has been very much cut away on this Patent very much diminishing the value of many and indeed most of the lots, the principal value of some of which consisted therein; and many lots will probably be still objects of Plunder among some the settlers unless carefully attended.

                                          Seth Herrick."

The accompanying chart, though it bears no date, gives numbers which correspond with the following list of land owners.

273. William Sullivan's lot,
274. Nath. Riches lot.
275. P. Downs lot,
276. Joseph Wardwell's lot,
277. Abner Bucknall's lot,
278. Weldens lot.
279. Benjn. Stubbs lot,
280. James Stubbs lot,
281. John Kempton's lot 300 A. and 150 P. (This number is not marked on the chart but three spaces are left.)
282. Widw. Riches lot,
283. Vinal's lot,
284. Widw. Lombard's lot,
285. No name,
286. Esqr. Goodwins, 54 A.,
287. Bowlings lot,
288.
289. Sampsons lot, 94 A..
290. Goff's lot.
291. Vacant.
292. John Martins lot,
293. Esquire Jones' lot,
294. Johnsons lot 100 A.,

12

295. Low's lot,
296. Capt. Oakman's lot, 100 A.,
297.
298. Esq, Livermores lot,
299. Grants lot,
300. Capt. Samson's lot 100 A.,

301. Wm. McGlathry lot,
302. Blaisdell's lot 206 1-2A.,
303. Tobias Halley's lot 113-4 A.,
304. Wm. McGlathry lot,
305. Clark & Gridley's lot,

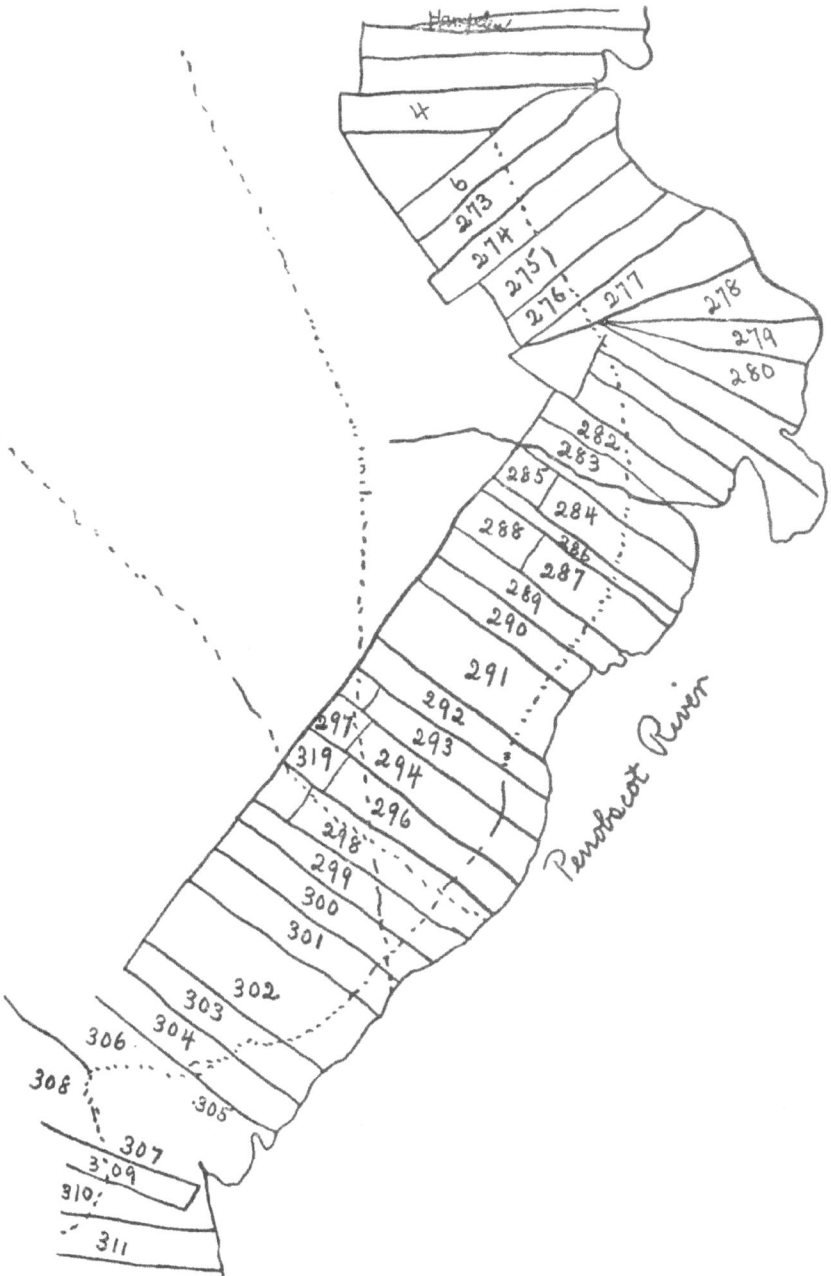

"This list is a description of lots surveyed in town of Frankfort A. D. 1808. It was taken from the original field books by James Malcolm for Archibald Jones Esq."

The following description of the survey of Mt. Waldo is as prophetic as it is interesting. "This large lot is on the noted Mount Waldo alias 'Mount Misery.' This noble emanance rises to a height capable of giving prospect of the sea and country as far as the eye can reach. The surface is generally of pretty smooth ledge covered by very little soil. * * * * The southern declivity is precipitate and in most places smooth and on the top is a flat of considerable extent and very wet swamp. —

"This Mountain can never be valuable for cultivation. It may, however, at some future day answer the same valuable purpose in the East as the famous Carter's Mountain in the South."

At this time the town of Monroe was known as Lee Plantation. Buckstown was across the river. Orrington and Hampden had received their names. In Frankfort were "flat rock falls," "Goose Pont," "Bauld Hill Cove" and the Plantation of Goshen. This last is a fertile, pastoral country and like the place in Biblical history still contains "some of the best of the land" in town. What we now call the Cove, was then North Frankfort.

Of the sixteen Maine counties we have had the good fortune to bear the names of four. A hundred and fifty years ago York County embraced the greater part of Maine. In 1760 the General Court of the Province of Massachusetts Bay defined the boundaries of a new county called Lincoln, with Pownalboro as the shire town. The records for the years following this date are now at Wiscassett. Again new boundaries were made and the county of Hancock was established. The act establishing this county was passed in 1789 and included Waldo Patent with other land. Penobscot became the shire town and all records for that time are now at Ellsworth. February 7, 1827, Waldo County was established with Belfast as its county seat.

The colonial governors had a hand in caring for our interests. Sir William Phipps, Governor Pownall, and Gage of Revolutionary fame, were the most famous of these. Among our constitutional governors are the familiar names of John Hancock, Samuel Adams, and James Bowdoin. The first state governor was William King.

II - Along the River

From early descriptions of the Penobscot river, we find that explorers hundreds of years ago were as greatly impressed by its beauty as are the summer tourists of to-day to whom it is the "Rhine of America." For, in the year 1556, when Andre Thevet, French scholar and priest, had visited the new world, the shores of both North and South America, and spent some days in Penobscot Bay, he says in his account of the voyages — "Having left La Florida on the left hand, with all its islands, gulfs, and capes, a river pre-

14

sents itself, which is one of the finest rivers in the whole world, which we call 'Norombeque,' and the aborigines 'Agoncy,' and which is marked on some marine charts as the Grand River. Several other beautiful rivers enter into it: and upon its banks the French formerly erected a little fort about twelve leagues from its mouth, which was surrounded by fresh water, and this place was named the Fort of Norombeque."

In the next century, Henry IV of France gave a patent of all the land between Cape Breton Island and the Hudson river to De Mong, who visited the country, exploring its coasts and rivers. He entered the Penobscot and afterward the Kennebec, where he took possession in the name of the King of France. All this territory was called Acadia. It was this voyage and this action of France which so alarmed the British Government, that in 1605, it fitted out the ship Archangel, to spy on the French, and to establish English colonies here. The captain of the vessel was George Weymouth who had seen many lands and also had been on an expedition in search of the Northwest Passage. He came to the Maine coast, among the islands, into the river, and finally landed near the town of Thomaston. On one of the small islands, probably Allen, he set up a granite cross, taking possession in the name of the King of England. They saw the river with "its gallant coves" in the month of June; and Rosier, the historian who accompanied the expedition, says "I will not prefer it before our river Thames, because it is England's richest treasure: but we all did wish those excellent Harbours, good deeps in a continual convenient breadth and small tide gates, to be as well therein for our countries good, as we found them here,

The Rhine of America

15

(beyond our hopes) in certaine, for those to whom it shall please God to grant the land for habitation: which, if it had, with other inseparable adherant commodoties here to be found; then I would boldly affirm it to be the most rich, beautiful, large and secure harboring river that the world affordeth."

At the celebration, 1905, in St. Georges and Thomaston, commemorating this voyage, a tablet was placed, bearing this inscription: —

THE EARLIEST KNOWN CLAIM OF RIGHT OF POSSESSION BY ENGLISHMEN
ON NEW ENGLAND SOIL.

Among the five Indian captives taken to England by Weymouth was one with whom boys and girls are familiar in their United States History. After falling into kindly hands abroad, he was returned to his native country: and Squantum, a Penobscot Indian, was the first to speak the word of "Welcome!" to the Pilgrim Fathers at Plymouth.

Up to this time I found no account of a traveler's coming to the section known as "old Frankfort" or what is the present town of Winterport. But, in 1722, in February, Colonel Thomas Westbrook came from the mouth of the Kennebec River with two hundred and thirty men to ravage the coast. It is said they came up the river as far as Marsh Bay and cast anchor. They were looking for an important Indian village and fort, probably Lett, near the present site of Oldtown. Going ashore, they began a march thro the forest, "still ascending the river." Finding the place deserted they returned to St. Georges. This must have taken them through the country hereabouts; and the first view of it must have been the same that the traveler has to-day as he leaves Bucksport and sails up the river, looking straight to the wooded sides of Treat's Point or Treat Hill.

The Indians had paddled up and down the river and perhaps touched at this shore, but I find no account of the white man's footstep, excepting the Westbrook expedition in 1759. Eastern Maine was a wilderness. The fortification of the St. John's river left the Penobscot a pathway by which the French might carry on their hostilities. For this reason, none had dared make a home on its banks.

Pownall, the royal governor of Massachusetts, like his predecessor, had long urged the building of a fort on this river. In his message he says: "The enemy have now no outlet to the sea but thro the river Penobscot, the door being shut in every other part. These lands ought to be in our possession." It was finally decided to take possession of this river. So Governor Pownall came with four hundred men to erect a fortification. This was in the same year that saw Quebec, Ticonderoga, Niagara, and Crown Point captured by the British: and thus France forfeited all claim to northeastern North America.

The governor and his party landed at what is now Fort Point and left some men there. With over a hundred men he ascended the river to explore. They landed above Brewer a few miles, and with ceremony buried a leaden plate bearing this inscription: —

MAY 23. 1759. PROVINCE MASSACHUSETTS BAY,
DOMINIONS OF GREAT BRITAIN. POSSESSION CONFIRMED BY THOMAS POWNALL. GOVERNOR.

The party returned. A fort was begun immediately which was completed in July and named Fort Pownall. This opened up the whole of the river valley, which in the words of the governor had been "a den of savages and a lurking place for some renegade French." The commanders of the fort were Jeddidiah Prebble and son, Goldthwait and Col. Johnathan Buck.

A later message from the governor says that many settlers "wish to go to Penobscot and there should be no question about the title of their grants."

Among the men who helped to erect this fort was a Lieutenant Joshua Treat, a gunsmith by trade, who had been armorer at Fort Georges nine years before. Lieutenant Treat understood the Indian language and was valuable as an interpreter. A story is told that "he paddled up the river in a canoe with Governor Pownall and landed at the Sowadabscook stream in Hampden, where he acted as interpreter in a conference with the Tarratine Indians and introduced the governor to the old chief Modockawando, which conference ended all troubles with the Tarratines." Joshua Treat arrived at Fort Point where he remained and was one of the first actual white settlers on the Penobscot river. In 1774, Joshua Treat Jr. built a log house in Frankfort, lived there for about ten years, and then went to live at the "Point Farm."

There was at this time a "new plantation called Frankfort on the east side of the Kennebeck in the county called York."

The Jones History says that Winterport had "two log houses in 1766 — one on the site of the Sampson house and one on the McGlathry place. They were owned by Ephraim Grant and John Coulliard."

Mr. Jones says, "There was to be seen at this time (1766) the remains of a battery on high head supposed to have been built by Baron Castine; a hollow place has marked the spot until within a few years." None of the French manuscripts speak of the Baron's coming here. It was a hundred years before that he had come to the peninsula now bearing his name, "had erected a safe and commodious dwelling," and had taken to himself an Indian wife, Mathilde, daughter of the chief, Modockawando. Castine the younger made a voyage up the Penobscot when he was taking despatches to the Governor of Canada in 1709. There is no proof that he stopped here; — but knowing this bit of tradition, we read with more interest Longfellow's Baron of St. Castine, and Whittier's description of him in Mogg Megone.

At Abbott place, in this town, is a copy of Will H. Low's picture of this "wanderer from the shores of France." The picture is framed in old oak, left in the rough. It was cut from a log which was taken from the harbor at Castine by the late Noah Brooks and Dr. Edmund Abbott in the eighties. The log is supposed to be a piece of the old British ship St. Helena, which was sunk there in Revolutionary times.

The silent shores could tell many a tale, if they would, of noted people who have passed up and down the river: of travelers famed in story and tradition: perhaps of Champlain or of seekers for the fabled fort of Norombega.

About twenty years ago, while a small boy was playing near the ruins of an old wharf at the "lower village," at the foot of Mechanic street, he found a ring imbedded in the mud. The following description of it was given me by its present owner. — "It is a large one. The man or woman whose finger it fitted must have been of large stature. There was no stone, but a 'setting' for a miniature or for hair is plainly to be seen. I have always supposed there was a portrait or a glass to protect a lock of hair, because the place was so shallow. This is the inscription which is on the outside of the ring, in small capitals — inlaid with black enamel.

Miles— James— Ob. 7— Sept. 1749— Aet. 54.

The ring is divided into five scrolls of unusual length, each length being suited to the length of the word or date inscribed; it is quite heavy being solid gold."

It was probably a mourning ring and may have been lost when the British came up the river in '79 or 1812; or possibly it was washed ashore from some wreck.

Year after year the same changes of weather and season have taken place; and before a name was given to this town, here was the winter port for any craft.

Mr. Frances Le Baron Goodwin in his diary says

"1792 — Dec. 28 Capn. Oakman arrived from Boston and hauld in at his Landing to Winter. Sunday."

"1793 — Feb. 3, River froze over against my House low tides and continued until ye 6th."

"1794 — Jan. 4 — Charles Kempton hailed me as he went up to O. Point to winter — no letters from Plimouth."

To-day the weather wise say that "every seven years it freezes below the steamboat wharf." I found an account of the "severe winter of 1832—33 when the river and bay were frozen over so that people passed on the ice to the outermost islands in the bay. ' The writer adds that there has been "no winter comparable with this since the year 1772." In 1834—35 the bay was frozen down to the outermost Islands. Sleighs and sleds passed back and forth from the Main to Long Island in March. During such hard "freezes" there was racing of horses and the better sport of ice-boating. As late as 1904 there was a small fleet of ice-boats on the river.

A closed harbor does not necessarily mean inactivity of the river folk, for now the winter fisher must begin his work. By law he may begin to smelt in

October; but it is not until November that you find the fishers here and there on the ice, or in boats in open water.

In the spring the first blue streaks in the ice foretell a weak spot — a warning for all life to take to shore. There are eager watchings and predictions about what day the "ice will break up and go out." Almanacks and old memoranda are consulted to see "what day it was last year." A table showing the dates of its departure from the years 1818 to 1883 gives Apr. 23, 1847 as its latest date. With the rush and whirl of the freshet comes the ice. Logs, cut loose from the booms up river, come tumbling on to the shore. Driftwood is piled on the banks. And with the arrival of the first boat "up river" we may say that the dreary winter is at last broken. Year after year the first craft is gladly welcomed by the villagers.

Now the summer fisherman prepares for work. If a shad fisher, he must go at evening up the river, drop his net from the boatside, and drift down with the tide. According to old accounts, these fish were plentiful in 1800, and in the fifties boatloads of them were hauled. A few of the best were sold at five cents apiece and the rest were taken by the farmers for fertilizer. To-day we pay twenty-five cents apiece for them.

Ice Boating on the Penobscot

At this season, too, the salmon fisher must build his weir and begin work. In early deeds mention is made of "salmon fisheries" and "salmon privileges." Rosier says, — "Here we saw great store of fish: some great leaping above water, which we judged to be salmons": and "fisheries" were given as an in-

19

ducement for settlers to come here. That salmon was considered a luxury in those days is attested by this extract from a diary in 1792:

"Captain C. came here forenoon and took a bite Broild-Salmon."

The Goodwin diary tells the sad fate of an Indian in a salmon weir near here.

"1792 — June 16 — Whittam found a birch canoe in his weir upside down."

"20. John Bowlin found a Drownd Indian in his Salmon Net and called the Neighs together and took him out examined and buried him found no marks of violence about him. It was the opinion of all present that he was Drowned, there was no Coroner in the Town.

"July 1. The Indians related to the one Drowned came and opened the Grave and found the corpse so far consumed that they covered him anew and placed a stone to his head and feet and made a Cross and painted it red and blacked the ends of it and placed it to his head. Crossed themselves and went home — they gave Bowlin the Cannow that Whittam picked up —

The dead Indian's name was Lieuene —"

A few years ago while looking for some graves on a point above the Bolan place, I came across one much larger than the others with rough stones at "head and feet." Later, on a second visit there, it was a strange coincidence that the ghostly stalks of the beautiful Indian pipes were growing on the same grave.

The last picture I find of the river in old times is the following taken in substance from the Frankfort Gazette in 1855 —

"Frankfort is one of the most beautiful of all New England villages. It is at the head of winter navigation, on one of the noble rivers of the world. It stretches for a mile along its banks which rise with a gentle inclination. It is dry, airy, healthy, and surrounded by a most beautiful and diversified landscape of fields, forests, waters, and mountains."

III - Natives of the Soil

While we are considering the discoverers, explorers, and the names they gave to the country, we should not be forgetful of the people whom they found here. Nearly all of eastern North America as far south as Cape Hatteras was known as the Algonquin country, and all the tribes of Indians living between the Penobscot River and the Piscataqua were known as the Abena'kis — a name changed by foreigners to Abnaki, Abenaqui, and Abenaques. The tribe occupying the Penobscot valley bore the name of Tarratines. In 1754 all of the Abenakis except the Penobscots had withdrawn to Canada. Very little can be found about the Indians who occupied this immediate vicinity. We can only judge of their disposition and customs by what we read of the Penobscots in general. In 1604, Champlain says, "Contrary to what might have been expected we found scarcely any inhabitants dwelling on the borders of the Penobscot. Here and there were a few deserted wigwams which were the only marks of human habitation."

One of the most powerful of the eastern sagamores was Modockawando, chief of the Penobscots. Historians say the prisoners of war held by this chief were remarkably well treated. He passed to the happy hunting grounds about 1698 and was succeeded by Moxus. Other chiefs were Orono, Loren, and the halfbreed Castin the younger. Orono is represented as a man of exemplary character, and is reputed to have been the son of the Baron de St. Castin. The town of Orono, in Penobscot County, commemorates his name.

Loren was an eloquent speaker at Falmouth when the Dummer treaty was signed.

Speaking of Anselm, Williamson says he always stood for peace. "It was in him both policy and pleasure to promote peace with the English. And, in several instances where they had treated him with abuse, he gave proofs of forbearance worthy of a philosopher or Christian's imitation." The English treated him as a friend and entrusted to him the mission of conducting Major Levingston thro this wilderness from Port Royal to Quebec. He also held a commission from the French King as second lieutenant of the navy.

In the 17th century the Indians had been visited by French missionaries. They had welcomed these, and had even employed French instructors from among them; and when, in a conference at Penobscot, they were asked to drive out the Catholic teachers, they refused to do so.

After the destruction of the fort and dwellings at Oldtown, by Westbrook, the Indians had made a small settlement of about fifty huts at Bangor. Again the English came as destroyers; for in 1725, Heath marched from the Kennebec, set fire to the settlement, and the Indians fled to the surrounding forests. Many again returned to Oldtown; and in June a few chiefs under a flag of truce went to the trading house at St. Georges, Thomaston, to sue for peace. Even on this mission one of the number was killed by the English.

In the same year, four sagamores of Eastern Maine met at Boston to confer with the authorities as to trade, the boundaries of their hunting grounds, etc. After a month's discussion the English gained their points, — first, possession of all the land they claimed; second, control of all trade. In December, the treaty known as the Dummer Treaty was signed. A copy of this is in the archives in the Boston State House. As only four sagamores were present another meeting was held at Falmouth, Maine; and in the presence of forty chiefs representing Maine, Nova Scotian, and Canadian Indians, it was again signed, July 1726, by Lieutenant Dummer and by twenty-seven sachems.

When in June 1755, war was declared against all the Indians in Maine, the Penobscots were excepted, and the government offered to take into its army all able bodied men of the tribe. They were asked to join the marching army of three hundred men, to scout through eastern Maine and protect the eastern frontiers, and were to have full pay as soldiers and officers. The government would care for invalids, women, and children. But they did not meet these advances and were afterwards forbidden to come to any of the forts or settlements in the province, for trading or for any other purpose. In November, they were declared "enemies and rebels," and "a Bounty and Encouragement" was to be "given and paid out of the public treasury for every Penobscot Indian Prisoner Brought to Boston and for every scalp."

The Penobscot Indians were the most peaceable of all the eastern tribes, and yet there is naught to boast of in the treatment they received at the hands of the English.

Judge Goodwin of this place became Superintendent of Indian affairs. He was appointed after the Commonwealth, in 1796, had purchased of the Indians nine townships on each side of the Penobscot, to prevent any trespass on Indian land. The Bangor Commercial says "A resolve of the legislature passed June 18, 1803, made it his duty to assist the tribe in using and improving their lands and property, in making contracts, in collecting their deeds and in preventing depredations on their wood lands, and requiring him to render upon oath an annual account of his doings. All contracts made with the tribe were to be void, unless first approved by the agent, and any one who trespassed upon its lands, forfeited treble damages, with double costs." This became the agency of which he was made superintendent which in the course of twenty years became an object of considerable competition among rival candidates. In 1807, he was superseded by Dr. Horatio G. Balch of Bangor.

Mr. Goodwin's diary mentions some of his dealings with neighboring Indians.

"Aug. 3, 1796. Daniel Davis returned from Bagwaduce and called here in the afternoon Drank Tea &c left here about sundown and went on to Condeskeg that night and the next day held their treaty with the Indians.

"Many Gents from Bagwaduce were there & Capt. Samson & wife from this place — my hay was all down & therefore could not attend said Treaty.

"Aug. 11, 1796. Read a letter from D. Davis excusing his not Callg & informing me of his success in Treatg with ye Indians. Oct. 7, 1801. Went to Condeskeg & Dupee & Esq. A. men to go down to Wheeler's Mills on board Capt. Kempton & get the Indian Corn &c bring it up to Condeskeg to deliver out to the Indians according to order from Q. M. Genl which I completed by (and) Returned Sat night making 4 days of myself besides all other Helpers."

In dealing with the Indians here, December 1799, he went out to see a settlement of Indians who were about to be routed and made peace between them and the owner of the land.

"Jan. 3, 1800. Gave Esq. Oxhorn an Indian chief 2 advertizements respecting cutting Logs on Indian Land."

These last two entries and the story of the dead Indian in the salmon weir, are the only written records left of the men who roamed through these forests thickly wooded with oak and pine, forests where the bear wandered at will — forests through which a traveler could make his way only by the Indian trail or spotted trees. Mr. Mitchell says the place is not located where they would choose to live long; it would always be merely a camping ground. They would live either "up river," or down at "salt water." This would be used as a tavern or an inn, a mere stopping place.

In conversing with an Oldtown squaw I learned that her aged grandfather, Pierre Mauly, with many others had lived here long ago. She is now eighty, and the grandfather must have been ninety at his death. He had told her that before any priest had worked among them they lived here. They came down in bark canoes; wintered and summered in bark wigwams; and lived by hunting, fishing, and digging clams.

The road just below the Guide Board Hill curves around a flat, one side of which is bordered by three parallel, oblong hills. As children, we always pretended that these hills were the graves of Indian giants. But tradition has it that long before any settlement was made here and before the first approach of any whites, this flat was the site of an Indian village. As it is near Flat Rock Falls, and the Catamawawa stream, and not far from the river, its situation naturally would have made it a favorite resort for them.

A few relics have been dug up here and there; a few stories are still preserved among us: but it is strange that no locality in this village bears an Indian name.

It is said that there was an old Indian burying ground on High Head. Shells have been washed from its clay banks, and at one time, human bones were found there. Under miscellaneous expenses in the town report for 1868 is this item. — "Pd. P. McShea for burying human bones found on High Head— $1.00."

The body of an Indian, with a bow and arrow, was dug up some years ago near the Cove. These were buried again, this time under an apple tree, which, the story goes, refused thereafter to bear fruit.

Six years ago, two men were walking on the beach at Oak Point when they saw something which they took for the end of a cannon protruding from the side of a bank. As it was in this vicinity the flagship Warren was destroyed in 1779, they were of course excited, and thought a great discovery had been made. On examination, the cannon end proved to be a copper kettle which covered a human head. The body was in a sitting posture upright in the side of the bank. The hands, each grasping a tomahawk, were placed on the knees. The flesh crumbled to dust at the touch, but the bones remained. Numberless strings of beads encircled the neck. These beads, strung on some twisted material, were of two kinds, — thin disks of shell alternating with beads of white pipe clay of various sizes, and cylindrical in shape. Lossing says, "Wampum is made of the clear parts of the common clam shell. This part being split off, a hole is drilled in it, and the form which is that of beads known as bugles, is produced by friction. They are about half an inch long, generally disposed in alternate layers of white and bluish black, and valued when they become a circulating medium, at about two cents for three of the black beads or six of the white."

The bank where the Indian was found has little hillocks on its side, indicating that possibly more bodies might be found there. This method of burial was common among the tribes: as they thought departed spirits would "have the same wants and occupations in the land of souls."

Our town is not wanting in its story of buried treasure. On the land now owned by Mr. Hoxie, and near his cottage at the shore there used to stand a large oak. An Indian burying-ground was formerly located here. Nothing now marks the spot, but twenty years ago rude stones were found there. It is rumored that money was also hidden. The treasure was supposed to have been buried in a copper kettle; and believers in its reality, and seekers for the prize were not few. A few bones have been the only reward for the searchers.

About forty years ago the Indians made a settlement at Hardy's Point, where they lived "off and on" for eight or ten years. I am told that one brave wooed and won his bride here and that the wedding took place at the Point. Among those who came here were John Loren, Old doctor Joe Sockabasin, Swassin Franceway, Peter Nicola and Frank Loren. The last named is better known as Big Thunder whose death occurred in 1906 at Oldtown. For a number of years before his death he had lived there, where he entertained many visitors with his relics and his stories of Indian customs. On one occasion when showing a scalplock he was asked if he approved of the custom of scalping. His answer was the gentle rebuke, "Madam, never take what you can't give."

On a recent visit to the Island I mentioned some of these names to an old Squaw. She too had camped in old Frankfort and is one of the few left at Oldtown who still clings to the native language. She shook her head, repeating each name after me in her soft Indian tongue. "Joe Sockabasin, no, he all dead — they all gone."

Many were attracted here from Oldtown because of the excellent hunting and the plenteous supply of ash for basket weaving. The sweet grass was not used then, as no fancy baskets were made. They must all be strong and useful in order to be salable, — "clothes baskets, market baskets, bushel baskets, peck baskets, egg baskets and bunnit baskets." This last kind, I presume, was the nearest approach to anything fancy in those days.

Part of the time they lived in the open field, and later moved to the southern side of the Point where they "limbed" the pines up for several feet and made a clearing for their tents. The ground was covered with pine spills; no sun shone through in summer; and the winter snow could scarcely sift through the thick branches.

The sounds of the war dance and war whoop were not unheard, yet none of the six or seven white families who lived on the Point ever found the red man anything but a good neighbor.

Sweet grass is now found above and below the steamboat wharf and by the Oaks. It was this which attracted the Indians, in early days, to stop at the oaks on the way "down river" to sell baskets.

No doubt Low's Brook had the same attraction for them that it had for the small boy of the town. It was a good fishing place. The brook was famous for trout; and in the spring, when the smelts went up the brooks to spawn there was joy in the heart of any youth who could repair thither with his dip net and "scoop" them up, or even make a good catch with his hands.

The camps were interesting places in later years to children on their way home from school. They liked to talk with the squaws, watch them weave the baskets, and perhaps have strips to weave of their own. They liked to play with the little pappooses, or watch for the men coming in from a day's tramp with bundles of ash on their backs. It was fun to sit by the hour watching them pound the ash from which they stripped material to make baskets. Any boy was glad to gather driftwood and do an errand which might bring in return a fine bow and arrow.

About fifty years ago the families at Whig street came and stayed all winter. The old grandmother who used to beg for cold victuals is not forgotten. Her gratitude was always shown by, "Thank you, sister, much obleeged." There were old Mollie Mollasses — Mollie Balarsic in Indian language — the Tippetoes, Joe Neptune, and Mary Francis. At that time they came in large numbers — canoe after canoe coming down the river, fifty or sixty at a time.

These camps were busy places, too, and often were crowded with visitors who bought baskets, or perhaps carried cold food to the Indians. It was not strange to see them on our streets in native costume. A man generally wore a feathered head dress and brilliantly colored blankets fastened about the neck. The squaw's costume consisted of a loose cloth dress and a tall felt hat adorned with feathers. Often they knocked at some door to trade, — possibly to buy peas or pork. Sometimes they were given shelter for the night. Wrapped in blankets, they were perfectly satisfied with a resting place on the kitchen floor. "Many an old squaw has stayed in this house all night;" reflected the owner of one of our homesteads.

Some may remember how young people used to gather around an old squaw, who, looking over her greasy pack of cards till she came to the right one, would say, "Light 'plected felly haas good heart f'r yeou, mees!"

Joe Mitchell was the last one to camp here with his family. His father, old Dr. Joe Mitchell, had been at Hardy's Point years before, and it seemed quite fitting that his son, a basket maker, should choose this town for a home. His family consisted of Mary, his wife, and Tommy, son of a previous marriage. They took a house here, and he was a citizen of the town for thirteen years. Eight children were born, several of whom attended the public school until 1905, when Mr. Mitchell returned to Oldtown with his family.

The children are named Stella D, Joseph D, Wanita D, Lodgie D, Phynne, Francis Rayne, Louis, and Zine. Joseph was known as little Joe to distinguish him from his father. Lodgie was named for the Howard Lodge of Masons, the Winterport lodge of which his father had become a member. The name "Phynne" is written "Fine" in the town record. Her advent into the world was with such comfort to the mother that when the doctor asked what the baby's name should be, Mrs. Mitchell said "O fine, I had such easy time." So Fine the name stands, altho the family spell it Phynne. Later she was baptized with the Christian name, Eliza. There is a new baby, born at Oldtown, named Flora. The middle initial of every name is D, which stands for Daylight, a family nickname. Mr. Mitchell's father was an early riser — up before the day — so he was given the name Daylight. His children and grandchildren take this name for life unless some one distinguishes himself. Then some friend or plajnnate may choose to call him by some descriptive term and his children will bear the new name.

Members of the tribe still go down to salt water and return again to their island home. To-day there are no braves, but in 1760 the river valley was ruled by sixty warriors. In 1780 there were four hundred and fifty-nine Indians at Oldtown. The number has now decreased to less than four hundred, of whom, only perhaps less than fifteen are full blooded. It seems a pity that their customs should be forgotten, that no traces of native costume should remain, and that in a few years not one will be left here who can speak the Algonquin language.

IV - At The Water's Edge in Old Days

The town of Winterport is thirteen miles from Bangor, the head of navigation, and forty-seven miles from the ocean. The river is a little over a fourth of a mile wide here; from the wharf at the foot of Ferry Street to the one on the other side, it is 1251 feet 6 inches and at high water it is 1684 feet. These measurements were taken on the ice in 1904, by Roger Sherman Rundlett and Seth H. Morgan.

In depth it varies from three and three-fourths to five and a half fathoms. These soundings were taken at mean low water. The river here is a little salt, at high water it is quite brackish, and in winter the shell ice on the shore has a slightly saline taste.

Just north of Bald Hill Cove and running a little southwest is the line which separates the towns of Winterport and Hampden; it also separates the counties of Waldo and Penobscot. This line follows the middle of the river running south; so that the ferry takes us from Waldo into Penobscot County. This river came very near being the western boundary of a county by the name of New Ireland which was to have had Castine as a capital. This was an attempt made by the British government to colonize the country between the Penobscot and St, Croix rivers under the name of New Ireland. The plan was abandoned on account of some doubt as to the right to the soil.

A survey of the river at this point was made in 1873 and 1874. Alexander Longfellow, brother of the poet, was then in the service. His name appears on the old Commercial House registers and he often was a guest at the house of the Honorable T. Cushing and of Albert Kelly, Esquire.

From Bucksport, the river pursues a northwesterly course till it broadens into Marsh Bay, which is about a mile and a quarter wide from Treat's Point to Drachm Point. The reach runs about northeast and southwest up past the village. The channel is an easy one for sailors as there are no rocks or falls and the current is swift here only at the spring tides. The rise and fall of the tide is about twelve feet; but it has been known to rise twenty-six feet, which is four or five feet above the wharf.

The shore line has changed greatly in twenty years. The water front from Eveleth's to McKenney's wharf is made land. The foundation was of logs covered with dirt. There used to be sandy beaches, but sawdust from the up-river mills has been deposited all along the shore and has covered these except in one or two places. Thirty or thirty-five years ago no grass grew on the shore at the foot of Ferry street or between the wharves, and at low water ships could be hauled far up into the dock. The line at the steamboat wharf must have changed considerably; for the last vessel built here, the Samuel Larrabee, was sent off the stocks at the west end of the group of buildings now standing on that wharf.

There were some large areas of marsh grass, and at present a few field marshes are left below Hardy's Point. This grass is still cut in the Kelly field and on the Hacket shore. The sale of it must have been an important item in early days; salt marshes and thatch beds are named in old deeds, and the harvesting of it was an event worthy of note in old diaries: for salt hay was excellent fodder.

At the Shore

Nearly every small cape or inlet is favored with a name — either that of some old settler or one chosen from its natural features.

Drachm Point is across from Marsh Bay on the Buckport side. It is a long point extending far out into the bay: and the Geodetic Survey chart of 1899 shows a series of banks under the water south from the Point, which bears the name Frankfort Flats. In the spring and fall many old scows may be seen here, whose owners are getting sawdust to be used as a fertilizer. All crafts of any size coming up river must make a big circle and keep well to the left of the two red buoys marking the channel, which is very narrow at this point.

Returning to the Frankfort shore south of the town we find Treat's Point and Hardy's Point. As we go up river we see Kenney's or Atwood's Cove, Kempton's Cove, Oak Point, Stubb's Point, Bald Hill Reach, and Bald Hill Cove. When we speak of Oak Point to-day we mean any part of the point lying across from Buck's Ledge.

When the first settlers came, of course the earliest mode of travel was by water, and some means of access to the shore was necessary. For this purpose rude structures called "landings" were built by many of the landowners, either for mere convenience in getting ashore or for commercial purposes.

I found one mentioned as early as 1792. "Dec. 28 Cap'n Oakman arrived from Boston and hauld in at his landing to winter Sunday." This one was probably somewhere on the shore just above Washington street, for Captain Oakman had taken up land in 1787 in this locality. He had come to the wilderness to buy wood lots, and to cut and sell wood. The same little sloop which brought him here made frequent voyages to Boston with wood for the cargo, and now and then carried passengers or his family. Miller Johnston had a landing, replaced later by a small wharf or abutment which was washed away in the seventies.

In 1793 there was a landing at Eben Colson's by Oak Point and a Miss Gibbs had a small wharf near there.

About 1800 Oak Point seems to have been the business portion of the town. John Kempton had purchased three hundred acres of land in the spring of 1793. He chose a good cove and later built his wharf at its head. His two-story house, built on posts driven into the ground, was near the wharf. The upper story was his home, and the basement contained a store from which he paid the men in his employ. The first shipbuilding in the vicinity was done at this wharf. Two vessels were built here. The first was the Cynthia, one hundred and fifteen tons. The second one was on the stocks and partly built in 1812. When Mr. Kempton knew that the British were coming up the river, he burned her on the ways to prevent her from falling into their hands. Probably Mr. Kempton shipped lumber from here too; for Sept. 11. 1796 "Capt. Richard Calley of the Brig Fair America loaded in Oak Point Gove with spruce spars." She "left this place 12 o'clock for Philadelphia, a fair wind and tide. — Capt'n Stubbs of Buckstown went with him."

Near the Kempton wharf was a brickyard which, it is said, employed twenty men. This was owned by a Miss Gibbs about whom little is known except that she was well-to-do and the people of the neighborhood called her the witch. In July, 1790, she "raized a two-story Gamble Roofed House." It must have been a big venture in those days for a woman to take up a habitation in the wilderness, in view of the helpless beings women were held to be; and it is not strange that she was looked upon as a witch. She stands alone as the first woman landowner in these parts, and we still hear of "Sal Gibb's pint."

There were Thompsons who had a wharf at Oak Point, and in 1812 they too had a ship partly built which was never launched.

An appraiser's description of land reserves to David Stubbs the free use of the wharf, landing place and road to and from it as used in 1840.

By 1802 a wharf had been built by a Mr. Hall at the entrance to Low's Brook. Mr. Hall was a dealer in West India Goods — Wild Irish Goods, as they were sometimes called — and remains of his store and wharf were to be seen as late as '44.

Enoch Sampson crossed over from Buckstown In 1793, settled on land which is now the center of the village, built a store and later a wharf. It was in 1779 after a naval encounter at Castine, that one of the British ships in her retreat up river, was sunk off Sampson's ledge. Afterward she was visited by a diving bell and some iron articles were recovered.

Perhaps one of the most interesting landings is the old McGlathry wharf. William McGlathry came up from Camden in 1798 or 1799, bought land in Frankfort, and settled at the southern part of the town. He was interested in trading and built a wharf with the usual storehouse. It was located at the head of the dock south of the present Eastern Steamship wharf.

At the present time, from this dock is the ruin of a long extension built parallel with the steamboat dock. Whether this, too, was built by Mr. McGlathry is a question. Some say that it was, and others that the first storehouse at its head was burned. The building, which had been stored with lime, was flooded at high tide and subsequently burned. Others say that Mr. Little built it, which seems quite possible as the two families were related, and a company wharf might have been a convenience.

The wharf was once in the hands of the Union Company, and later was hired by Treat and Company who did a big coopering business. In those days the place was lined with cooper shops and store houses. There were four cooper shops, two of which were known as the "red one," the "white one." Probably thirty-five men worked here. After Treat and Company, the firm of Joshua and Charles Treat continued the same business. The latter member of this firm has for many years been Treasurer at Washington, and people fortunate enough to possess United States bills or bank notes will find his autograph on each one.

A man named William Dewey had a shop at the head of this small wharf. This "Uncle Dewey," as the boys called him, was an interesting character. He came here from Springfield, Massachusetts; and it is said that when he was a little the worse for rum, he always swore by S-f-d. In his day we boasted of an artillery company; and one day his tall lank figure was seen coming up the street, clad in military costume, and bearing a loaf of bread aloft on the point of a sword. When questioned as to its significance his reply was, "Oh, that's life on the point of death."

The McGlathry wharf was again visited by fire, and one winter night the storehouse and all the shops were razed to the ground.

The little old wharf has been owned for the last forty years by Mr. Joseph Moody, who for most of the time has done coopering, so that it retains its name "cooper shop wharf."

This locality also has its story incident to the war of 1812. The British vessel, Kertusof, with Captain Alexander Millikin of this town as prize master, was brought here. She was loaded with cocoa which had been sold at auction in Boston. Mr. Thorndike, one of the Ten Proprietors had bought it. He happened to be here at the time of her arrival, so the cargo was discharged into the McGlathry store house — where F. W. Haley's store is now — to be disposed of later. However, rumor of the approach of the British caused it to be hastily removed. From this point stories of the cocoa are many and varied, some of them perhaps more interesting than truthful. It was concealed in many places all through this section, and even to-day we may expect to find a handful of it hidden in any unheard of place. Perhaps the whole incident might be fittingly called the "Frankfort Cocoa Party."

This occurred just before the British had ascended the river to capture the Adams at Hampden. A letter dated August 1814 mentions the arrival of the Adams. "The 22nd U, S. States Frigate Adams arrived at Frankfort from a 9 months crus which was quite a site in the Place. She got on shore, met with Damage, came into Repair."

What is now known as Eveleth's wharf is built out over the end of the old Dean Wharf, the former being at about the center of the present one. At that time the water must have flowed high over the newer dock, for all this land along the river road is made land.

Tisdale Dean, its owner, a trader from Taunton, Massachusetts, was an early settler. In 1802 he had a store just at the head of the ferry way on the north side. The ferry way, or street, was then "understood to be 3 rods measured from the stairs of Charles Stern's Store."

In 1806 Mr. Dean moved his business across the way into a building on the Stokell site, and became the junior member of the firm, Andrews, Ware, and Dean. They carried on an extensive trade, barter in those times, exchanging our wood products of oak barrel and hogshead staves, rift clapboards and shingles, spruce knees, bark, etc., for provisions, West India and domestic goods. Rift clapboards were split by hand and shaved with a draw shave or frow. All large knees come from the roots of large spruces, but in small boats oak limbs can be used. Knees are now replaced by metal braces or trusses but a few may be found to-day on corners of our wharves.

The firm built the Orion, a vessel of a hundred and fifteen tons, just a hundred years ago. Mr. Andrews afterward built a vessel, the William, for his son of that name, and probably she sailed from this wharf on her voyages to Cuba. Here, too, Captain Andrews returned from his own foreign voyages.

Mr. Dean married Mary, the daughter of Mr. Andrews, and they went to housekeeping with "Square" Shaw on the hill. Mr. Andrews and his son-in-law transacted much business together, purchasing a home for the young couple. The lot extended from the river to the county road and a part of it was a pennyroyal field when purchased. The street now bearing his name was near its northern boundary, and a line at the present Willow street was the southern. At the time of its purchase in 1825, a house and barn stood on the lot. The former has since been known as the old Dean house and remained standing until within a few years. It was altered after its purchase, from a flat roof to the sharp roof of its later days.

Neighbors were not near, and from the upper windows an unobstructed view far up and down the river was to be had.

This must have been a spacious dwelling for those days; and that its interior was comfortably and even handsomely furnished is recalled by a few and shown by some substantial pieces of furniture still preserved. The visitor who lifted the brass knocker was always welcome by this family. According to custom he was received in the kitchen, where he perhaps found the family — three boys and three girls — gathered around the big, open, driftwood fire. The fireplace was most attractive, but comfort was brought by the big box stove at the other end of the room.

A granddaughter recalls an occasional glimpse of the best room: wall paper with large figures of people riding horse-back, carrying drawn bows, ready to

The Old Dean House

shoot; a large old-fashioned sofa with turned ends; the best parlor mirror, large and oblong, with heavy gilt frame, its only ornament being a raised gilt flower at the top. Probably here also was the library: such books as History of Charles Mandeville, a Sequel to Lady Julia by Mrs. Brook; Ambrose and Eleanor or the Disinherited Pair; Tale of the Revolution by an Officer; Children of the Abbey; Don Quixote; and Pilgrim's Progress.

It was a great treat to each grandchild to spend a night at the old house and sleep in the high, four posted bed with its curtains and valence. It was fun to sleep in a bed that had felt the warming pan. The attic was a fine place to play. On the way thither there was one door that must always be opened and peered through long and wistfully — the room where grandmother kept her jelly.

In the attic were treasures untold: a cloth loom where the linsey-woolsey was woven, a spinning wheel, flax wheel, swifts and reel, bespeaking busy fingers.

Those who have access to the public library today may now and then look into the kindly face of Tisdale Dean; for his photograph is on the book plates of books presented by his daughter, Elizabeth Dean Johnston.

A man influential in town affairs; a Whig, yet for thirty years serving a Democratic town as its treasurer; interested in church; a friend of children: he was, in the words of a neighbor, "one of the best men that ever lived."

V - River Crafts

This settlement was destined from its beginning for a shipping community; its situation half way to the sea, a shore line supplied with coves and streams, and sites favorable for landing places, all explain the growth of a "river town" like old Frankfort. The men who chose an abiding place here were seafarers; deeds describe them as seamen, trader, mariner or captain. Their former homes, old Plymouth, Wellfleet, Bristol and Provincetown proclaim their natural inclination.

One chose his lot because it was good woodland; he could sell lumber; another could see in the oak groves future ships which would carry his lumber abroad and return from far countries bearing foreign products.

The prospect of a fortune on these hillsides, heavily crowned ridges and oak groves of the old forest attracted young men. They began life anew in an untried country as men went West to live in '49.

Their homes were log huts, each in its little clearing, their livelihood depending on the work of their hands. In some cases, money was saved and invested in a craft to carry their forest products to the world's market. He who possessed a sloop was accounted well-to-do. Nearly every settler bore the name of captain and either owned his own sloop or was master of one owned by his neighbor.

The river and its burden was their life. The coming and the going of ships was carefully noted.

"Sept. 11, 1792 a large Sloop went up the River the first vessel except Treat's Brigg for eight Days."

Now and then a vessel returned from the Indies or set out from here on a longer trip. Two arrivals in the same day must have been an event. The many purposes which early crafts served is shown by this entry in Judge Goodwin's diary, —

"Went on board Captain Carres Schooner and got a pair of shoes for my wife," "went on board Capt. Lewes Brig to carry a letter for Mr. Samuel Prince in Brinston Gt. Britain. My wife, child and myself went in afternoon over to Lewes House and spent the afternoon with him and his wife Captain Delano there."

Thus we know that while in port, early captains were postmasters and shopkeepers. We can well imagine the subjects of conversation during the call at Lewes' house; news of the world across the seas was exchanged for stories of local happenings; of plantings, road-making, ploughing of new land, building new homes and of visits to the sick, (for the writer was doctor as well as judge) while their wives sat near with knitting and spinning.

These vessels carried passengers, too. It is recorded that "Capt. Cunningham sailed for Boston with Col. Moore and Capt. Crosby passengers," and "Capt. O. sailed from here with his family on board."

That each passenger supplied his own luxuries is told in the following:

"1796 went down with my bed and chest in company with Abner Bicknal on board the fore top sail Schooner Two Sisters, John Dutch Master, Laden with wood and other lumber and bound for Boston." On the return trip "left Boston about 3 o'clock in the morning on board Cap'n James Treat with 19 Passengers on board bound for Penobscot."

An early trip from Plymouth to Frankfort is thus described.

"May 1796 Nath Kempton arrived at Plym. from Eastward Penobscot begun to unload Friday and sailed again for Penobscot with Chandler and myself on board. Left plim. at sundown Saturday and Sunday night at sundown we anchored at Portland — Hog Island Road — we had head winds all the time until the 19th we made to lay under the fore-sail two nights round Menhegin. After that made about a Dozen harbors and at Length arrived at Oak point ye 19th May."

One of our early traders who went to Boston twice a year for his stock "staged it" if he were in a hurry, but if not he went in a "coaster."

Among the small crafts commonly used on the river were the canoe, dugout, gondola, dory, and scow. Of course for age the bark canoe holds precedence. A dugout or log canoe was also used. This was simply a log hollowed out. It was propelled by a paddle. Our first ferry boat was such a one. This conveyance was used elsewhere in New England for in Holland's Bay Path — says, "You'd better scull your dugout over the drink again and go to Splittin' wood."

The gondola was not a Venetian craft but a flat bottomed boat used for carrying produce. Various corruptions of this word are gundalo, gundaloe, gundelow and gundalow; an old bill has for one item "Day's work on a Gundlo."

The same kind of boat that figures in Captains Courageous is used on the ferry to-day — "swaying with the sway of the flat-bottomed dory." The ungainly scow is still seen taking a "team across."

The primitive method of transportation for an animal was to tow the creature behind the dugout, — "Dec. 1, 1797 Got a sheep and a Lamb of Eldridge Towed Old Bonney."

Settlers were not long in availing themselves of the advantages of their surroundings and were soon at work contributing their small part to the building up of the merchant marine which the first Congress had so strongly advocated to the colonies.

An equipped yard was not a necessity then to carry on shipbuilding; but a man set up his own stocks, built his ship, and often took her to sea himself — master builder and master of the craft.

Oak Point has the honor of having the first vessel built in town, when Captain John Kempton built the Cynthia. Then in 1807 the Orion was built by Andrews, Ware and Dean.

In 1810 the Franklin was built at Frankfort. She was a schooner of 92 tons carrying 6 men. It is not known by whom she was built but Nehemiah Rich sold her to Samuel Kempton and Captain Kempton's letters give us a little idea of the Franklin's trials in the War of 1812. She managed to steer clear of the non-importation act and in February of that year was hound for Barbadoes. On her return she became a prisoner in Penobscot waters. But at the first opportunity the captain sailed out of the river with "2000 rails or more and an additional cargo of lumber."

During the following six weeks he was not heard from and a letter from a relative solicitous for his welfare closes with the hope that the "rest of the Penobscoters are getting their fill of Madisonian Republicanism." It is evident that the efforts of the "Champion of American shipping" were not appreciated in this quarter.

Again in January, 1814, Captain Kempton was embargoed in Penobscot river but by June he had reached Portland from which town he writes, "The enemy are destroying all the vessels in the coastway trade and I expect to be obliged to hall my Schooner up leave and Strip her and go home without her." On the day before Christmas of this same year the Treaty of Ghent was signed and in February of the following year the Franklin was detained for five days in the ice in Boston Roads. Captain Kempton writes,

"The first news I had from Bof was the joyful surlute of cannon from the forts in all Directions then followed by a lumination in the evening until ten at night, there was nothing but joy to be once more freed from the toils of war."

The Franklin was in existence in 1816 and made nine trips to Boston and the cape.

At least two vessels were built in Frankfort near the year 1825. The William was built and named for her captain, young William Andrews, who went some voyages to the West Indies. His death occurred in 1829. Then at the foot of Holmes street a full-rigged brig was built for Captain Arthur Childs. She was named the Nancy and Hannah. While on her first voyage, on her way to Cuba, lumber laden, she was overtaken by a squall in the Gulf stream and capsized. All hands were lost except two of the crew who were picked up and taken to London.

In his book on American Navigation, Mr. Bates says that from '46 to '60 were the most important years in the history of the United States merchant service; that these years saw the "deep sea tonnage mount to its highest fig-ure" and saw the "beginning of its melancholy decline." Boston surrounded by the busy yards of Salem, Newburyport, etc., was a center of the shipbuild-ing industry.

Throughout New England this prosperity was felt and here and there along the Penobscot shipyards appeared. In the '40s Frankfort village, too, felt this prosperity. Among the vessels of this period were the T. O. Thompson, Ruth Thomas and the Captain John. The Balloon was re-built here. In youth this craft had been painted bright blue so she was nicknamed the Blue Loon. The date of her construction is unknown but one of her masters, Cap'n Jack, said "she was old enough to vote in the fifties." She made many voyages to the West Indies and Canary Islands and spent her declining years in the ship hospital at Bucksport, her hull hauled up on the shore, one old mast still standing.

In '48 Treat and Company built two vessels at the Marsh, — the Nancy Treat, a bark, and the Ellen Maria, a brig.

This industry was prolonged by the discovery of gold in California and also by the Crimean War. During the latter, France and England both needing their ships for supplies, withdrew them from the ocean highway and left ocean commerce to be carried on in American bottoms; they also bought American vessels for transports. "As a result" Mr. Bates says "American ship-yards produced more tonnage than they had before or since."

So the palmy days of shipbuilding for us began in the 50s'. At the Marsh various members of the Treat family were in the business; and in the village there were five yards; the largest ones were Treat and Company's, Dunham's, and Williams's.

On their stocks Treat and Co., built the James Churchill in '55 and the Har-riet Churchill in '56; the Robin in '57, the M. A. Herrara in '58; the Alice and the Czarina in '59; the Alpine and the John Dwyer in '64; the George Treat and the Samuel Larrabee later.

The bark James Churchill was named for a Portland man, a shipbroker who did business in Cardenas. She was built for the South American trade. In '81 her name had been changed to Harlingen for she then belonged to a Holland firm, and hailed from the port of Harlingen.

The Harriet E. Churchill was wrecked in the outer harbor at Cardenas on her maiden voyage. At the same time the Ellen Maria chanced to be in that port. So it was decided to put all spars and top hamper of the Churchill on board her to be shipped to Winterport. The home bound vessel was to bring the crew of the disabled one while the captain and mate returned by steam-er. That spring on the fourth of March, there occurred one of the worst storms on our coast, so severe that no town meeting was held in the state of Maine on that day. The Ellen Maria sighted Cape Cod in a blinding snow storm and was driven ashore. The captain died on the gallant fo'castle and of the two crews only one man was left to tell the story. That was the mate of the Ellen Maria who came ashore on a mast, leaving the vessel and her wreckage pounding to pieces on the cape.

When the Robin is mentioned, the inevitable remark is, "Of course you know why that vessel was named!" This is the story which I have from the man who did the planking on the brig Robin. While she was being built a bird began a nest right between the Knight heads and raised four young ones. The men worked around her nest, planks passed over her but she didn't mind. One day I called Colonel Treat, the owner, to the scene and there lay the robin with four young ones. While takin' our noonin' one day the mother and four little ones flew away. Then the father built another nest on the starboard side and with his new mate reared four young ones more. Mr. Treat was so interested that he hung up the planking till the last one was hatched out. When the last wee bird came, we finished the vessel and she was named the "Robin."

She was a fine vessel, finished handsomely and was painted by John Pope, some of whose work still adorns a Winterport home. She was four months in construction, was built for Captain Frank Killman and carried six or seven men before the mast. She went on Cuban voyages and was one of the most successful vessels Treat & Co., ever owned. Like many owners in war time their vessels were put under English colors and by '70 the Robin had left the United States for good. She sailed to the Baltic sea, her captain had to forfeit her for a bottomry bond in a second Baltic port. She was alive in '81.

"And what did the Robin do then, poor thing?"

The M. A. Herrara was named for a Spaniard in Cuba. She was sold in Boston for South American and West India trade. She was finally lost on Cape May — ran ashore and never came off.

Treat & Co., generally had one ship on the stocks at a time but in '59, the Czarina and the Alice were both in construction. The former, designed for Russian trade, was named for the Emperor's wife. Her first voyage was an unhappy one. She went to Charleston, South Carolina, loaded with hay, at which port her future captain was to take her. Captain Dwyer sailed the Czarina to St. Petersburg. On the return voyage he put in to Shields, England, shipped a new mate and started for home. Some trouble arose among the officers and one morning the captain, second mate and steward were found dead, and the mate's body locked in his room. The cook was somewhat of a navigator and ran the vessel for the broadside of America. She was picked up and reported one hundred miles off Sandy Hook; an officer was put on board and brought her into New York. All of the crew told the same story, that the mate had killed captain and officers, then taken his own life. After that the Czarina was put in the Argentine trade, finally was sold to a Buenos Ayres firm and in later years was known as the Anna.

The second vessel built in '59, designed as a fruiter, was launched the Fischer. This was the name of a member of the West India firm for which she was built. The Civil War broke out, the firm refused to take her and she was left on Treat's hands. They put her under English colors, named her the Alice and sent her to the St. Lawrence, to the Bay of Chaleur, as a mackerel fisher.

It seems as if Alpine must have been a favorite name with Mr. James Treat for he was interested in three crafts by that name. The first was the brig, built by the Bone and Muscle Society, which the firm bought and launched After her first voyage out of the river she never again came to a United States port. She went to Rio Janeiro and thereafter engaged in dry trade, taking coffee to Marseilles and returning loaded with wine. She was finally sold in Hamburg.

At the time of her launching a second vessel was on the stocks which was also named the Alpine. She made many successful voyages and was finally lost in a gale off Cape Hatteras.

The John Dwyer was built during the war. The first master was Robert Killman. On one voyage he left her in Jacksonville and sent for his brother Frank, late of the Alpine to take her. Captain Frank Killman and his wife came — and for some reason did not sail immediately. While waiting in the outer harbor Mrs. Killman contracted the yellow fever — a little way out at sea her death occurred. Her body was placed on Orange Key on the Bahama Banks, to be taken away at some future time. The vessel proceeded to Buenos Ayres, found no business there, so consigned to go to Valparaiso, proceeded to Chincha Islands and loaded with guano for London. They took on the cargo at Chincha, and when six days out at sea the captain died. His body was buried in the hold and the mate was to take the vessel to London. As they ran up the English Channel a government steamer ran into the Dwyer splitting and sinking her, When a brother went later in the J. Churchill to get the body of Mrs. Killman, a storm had washed it from the reef, so that the captain, his wife and the ship all found the same grave.

The George Treat went to the West Indies and back to New York and Philadelphia on her first trip. Then she followed the same route of the John Dwyer and finally was sold to New York parties.

The last vessel built by the Treats was the Samuel Larabee. Captain William Thompson, accompanied by his wife took her to Savannah. There taking on a cargo of cotton she put out to sea sailing for Bremen and was never again heard from. It is supposed that she burned at sea.

"And men go down in their ships to the seas.
And a hundred ships are the same as one."

The brothers Isaac and George Dunham were shipowners as well as shipbuilders. Besides the Rich fleet they have turned off their stocks the Addison Gillbert, Daniel Sharp, Mary E. Long, Arabella, France, Lucy M. Collins, Eastern State, Speedwell, Reynard and Nonpareil.

The Addison Gillbert was a ship of 861 tons. In '81 she was reported as the schooner Uno and hailed from the Norwegian port of Stavenger.

The naming of some of these vessels is interesting. The Daniel Sharp was named for a New York gentleman who presented her with a set of handsome silk flags. The Arabella was named for Mr. Dunham's daughter, and the Mary E. Long for the daughter of a Boston gentleman.

In '56 the France was built and it is said that she was given that name because it was hoped the French government would buy her for a transport during the Crimean War. Mr. Dunham's daughter saw her in Havre in after years. Later she had been renamed the Goethe.

One writer says that "the swiftest of our ocean greyhounds of to-day awakens no such enthusiasm as did those of the Black Ball Line by their passages of eighteen to twenty days from the Hudson to the Mersey. Most of the high class packets were built at East River and only a few came from New England." The Nonpareil, built at the Dunham yards was for this line and became a sister ship to the Dreadnought. This latter was the champion of the Atlantic packet service and ran from New York to Liverpool. She was nicknamed the Wild Boat of the Atlantic, or the Flying Dutchman.

The construction of steam vessels, also the discovery of gold in California, brought about the building of the "celebrated Yankee clippers" as they were called. The largest vessel built in Winterport, the Spitfire, was intended for a San Francisco packet to run from New York around the Horn; but she went into trade and was wrecked on the English coast. Mr. Lindsey describes these clippers as "wonderfully beautiful" and "splendid racers" and adds that "not one is now afloat in ocean service."

The half completed Alpine was the last vessel built by Williams and Arey. Previously they had launched the Ben Willis, Barbadoes, Daniel Williams, Gibraltar, Lucinda Maria, T. O. Thompson and the T. A. Cunningham.

The Caroline E. Kelley, the John Henry and the Wild Pigeon were launched at the foot of Marine street.

We are told that the "decline of shipbuilding had set in several years before the first shot at Sumter" and that the final blow to merchant service was the coming of the Cunard steamers, altho a little building was done in the '70s.

In the Longfellow house in Portland hangs a painting by J. R. Tilton, "The Shipyard." This represents a half-finished vessel on the stocks, but dimly seen thro haze and mist. Thus we see our flourishing industry thro changing years. If standing on the Post Office steps some summer afternoon, when a brisk southerly breeze blows up the river, we can imagine seventy vessels in full sail — old and new, patched and worn, — making their way, we have a sight not uncommon half a century ago. Now it is a treat to see one in full sail — for in the busy rush of the age they are towed up — they cannot wait for the wind and tide.

Not the least interesting of the river crafts was the Good Ship Rover, a vessel which grew in the imagination of one of our old stevedores. Over and over again she was built and manned for the small boys of his neighborhood who gladly sawed and split his wood day after day for a yam about this remarkable ship. Even they did not fully appreciate her wonders till they had attained to manhood and retold of her marvels and exploits, in turn adding a little with each recital.

From the Post Office Steps Some Summer Afternoon

A definite idea of her size may be gained from this incident; one day just after she had rounded the Horn it became evident that something was wrong "up forrard." A young sailor was sent to investigate; on his return he was a gray-headed old man, so long had he been absent, for her bowsprit was way up in Aroostook County, Maine.

She went to New York to load with hard pine planks for Liverpool. The men put the planks in thro the port holes in New York and passed them thro the opposite ports on to the wharf at Liverpool.

The crews hailed from various countries. When the old man pictured the yards too high for man to climb, the small boy's question was satisfied by telling him that "a crew of ringtailed monkeys tended them sails," and in the main top was a "crew of cuckoons."

On the way out to sea one day a school of whales was encountered and they knocked a hole into her hold, the whole school was taken into her hold, repairs were made and the Rover proceeded homeward. This same hold was at one time loaded with magnesia in the lower hold and cambric needles between decks, all carefully stowed points up.

Among the accessories were a railroad, by which the officers could go aft; a telegraph, and the captain traveled around the deck on horseback. Truly the Rover was not an ordinary coaster.

It is said that the earliest steamers anchored in the river, while passengers and freight were ferried in small boats to the shore. The sound of the first whistle so alarmed one good elder that he rushed to his barn, seized his gun, expecting to shoot a panther. Other inhabitants were greatly alarmed thinking a man-o'-war was coming.

The first iron sea-going propeller constructed in the United States was the Bangor, built for the Bangor Steam Navigation Company and launched in

Wilmington, Delaware, May 1844. After her first trip between Boston and Bangor, she was burned in August at Dark Harbor, Islesboro. Alden Parker of Bangor, and later of Frankfort was her master.

The Old Bangor

The next year the Bangor was rebuilt at Bucksport, was purchased by the Government and renamed the Scourge. With her the Alvarado was captured at the commencement of the Mexican War.

Description of the Steamship, "Bangor."
First Iron Sea-going Propeller Steamer in the U. S.
Built by the Harlan and Hollingsworth Co.,
Wilmington, Delaware, In 1843—4.
When bought by the Government, was renamed Scourge.

The "Bangor" was the first iron sea-going propeller steamer constructed in the United States. She was begun in October 1843; launched in May of 1844, and was completed and delivered to her owners, the Bangor Steam Navigation Company, of Maine, in 1844. Her dimensions are as follows:

Length over all on deck, about 131 ft.
between perpendiculars   120 ft.
Breadth of beam   23 ft.
Depth of hold   9 ft.

This photograph shows her peculiar shape, particularly as to her bow and stern, and presents a well-marked instance of the type of construction in vogue at that period. It was, however, considered of a very handsome and graceful design by all the critics of that day.

She had three wooden masts, schooner-rigged, with bowsprit and jibboom, carrying a suit of eight sails.

Her accommodations were as follows: — The crew's quarters were located forward in the hull. The passengers were carried on deck in a commodious house fitted up in a style of elegance unusual in those days, and considered particularly handsome by her owners and builders. Upon the interior of this house was a comfortable saloon, surrounded by sleeping accommodations intended for night service. When built there were two deck houses upon the vessel, the third or forward house, as shown in photograph, having been added afterward. The galley, pantry, lamp and other rooms were located amidships. The pilot house was located aft for sea-going purposes, and had one room abaft for the use of the commander and pilot.

Her machinery consisted of independent twin screw propeller engines. The propeller wheels were of the Loper type. The boiler was of the type known as the "drop flue."

A custom house was here as early as 1853. In that year between August and December, seventy-eight vessels were recorded as cleared. Lincoln appointed Theophilus Cushing as collector of the port in 1861 and he occupied the southern part of the post office building. Captain George Dudley succeeded him in the office.

A report in 1862 gives foreign entries 15, clearances 27; the value of foreign exports was $5,160,055.

A paper of that time states that these vessels were all or partly loaded with articles of foreign production. A very much larger number was loaded with domestic produce for home ports, but these were not required to enter or clear. During the same year 90,000 bushels of potatoes and 12,000 bushels of barley were shipped. The potatoes went to feed the army, and the barley went to the French army in Mexico where it was fed out to transportation teams.

The port of customs was removed to Hampden and now Bangor is the port of entry for the district.

VI - Their Captains

In our village, one is so used to addressing a man as captain, that for the moment the significance of the title is forgotten. The captain is master — commander — no matter how small is his craft, his prestige is the same. For him a ship is built; but this compliment stirs not his pride nor touches his vanity one-half so much as when he can tell you some incident relative to his life as cabin boy or as one of the crew.

And when he has taken his last voyage the title still lives on the slate slab which marks his resting-place, unless mayhap he sleep at sea.

While most of his life is spent far from home, yet the various errands entrusted to his wisdom and the many offices which he must perform, amply fulfil all his duties as citizen.

Has he made successful purchases of clothing or of provisions while away? Then is his vessel converted into a store and visited by many customers on his return.

Perhaps while waiting in a distant port he has been visited by a father or mother and some message is entrusted to his care for a son or daughter in this far-away wilderness. He is paid the courtesy of "Politeness of Capt—" given the carefully folded sheet which is letter and envelope too, and his coming is eagerly awaited by those who know him for a trusty messenger.

What confidence is placed in his ability to choose articles for the house or even of wearing apparel; sets of dishes — twelve dozen dinner plates and others in proportion; a china tea set; table linen by the piece, bleached and unbleached. So careful was his selection that one piece has come down thro generations, mother, daughter and granddaughter — and is now treasured by the last of four Marys.

Choice of wall paper for the best room was a task slight in comparison with selection of silk for a bridal gown, or a fan for a gift. It was worth months of waiting to take the latter from its heavy pasteboard case — and behold it when spread — of English parchment whose front was a gorgeously painted garden, its back showing Eve in the garden while near by Pan is skipping to his pipes; its ivory sticks, exquisitely carved, were inlaid with pearl and silver.

When trading is over and the hundred and one errands incident to the home coming dispensed with, from the old sea chest in the corner of the cabin, the captain takes a bundle; with care he bears it home, lays it on the table — an offering to her who has been the home captain; perhaps it was a smoked glass pitcher from Dublin that took his fancy.

Then follow happy days to his boys — who may go daily to the vessel and help in the repairs and in the things that need attention before the next voyage; but if they become too boisterous in their play with him, this master of wind and wave, unequal to this task, must take shelter behind this threat "Boys, behave yourselves or I'll tell your mother of you."

He is a welcome guest to any family and an audience is never lacking to listen to the news and his sailor yarns — over cider and apples till the fire bums low.

Previous to the year 1808 the chief landowners in this plantation were the captains; Kempton, Rich, Lombard, Bolan, Johnston, Oakman, McGlathry, Sampson and Blaisdell. Three doctors, a few farmers and some lawyers had also taken up claims.

John Kempton, the pioneer of our shipbuilding industry was born in Plymouth, Massachusetts, in 1740. He came from a family of sailors and in turn followed their calling. A trip to the Indies, to the Maine coast; among its islands where he bought and sold land; or into Maine rivers completed his travels.

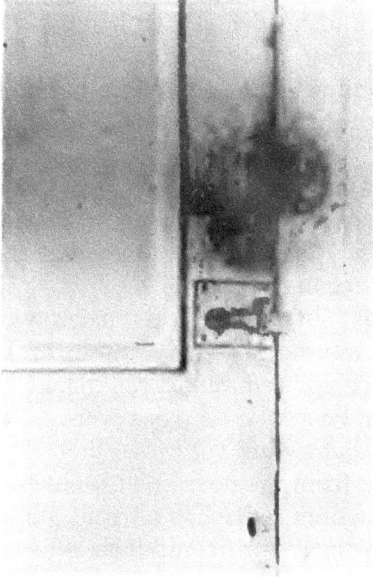

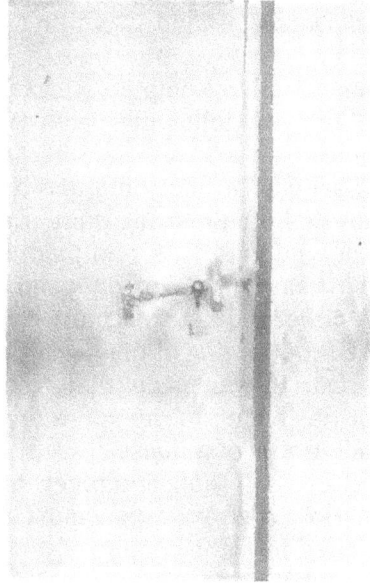

Door Latches, Bolan House

Evidently he was favorably impressed with the Maine country, for in the spring of 1789, Captain Kempton and Francis Goodwin "set off for the East-ward to look up farms to live on." They sailed into the Penobscot and at Oak

Point were attracted by the oaks and pines. Here they landed and tarried for a month with one William Colson. Mr. Kempton chose a spot on the hill overlooking a cove which now bears his name and there put up a rude log house. A small parcel of land was purchased, and he decided to bring his family here.

In June Captain Kempton with his friend returned to Plymouth and in August of the year following, again sailed to the eastward, this time to make it his home.

A wharf was at once built and a frame house set on piles near it. In 1773 Captain Kempton became quite a proprietary owner having purchased 300 acres of wild land. The sum paid was £137; as English money was then reduced in value, he had paid seventeen cents an acre.

This hitherto quiet spot must have been surprised at the busy days which followed the coming of the packet to its shore. At the first sounds of the ax a small clearing was made; then trees were spotted and a trail marked to the distant neighbors, to the shore or to the county way; trees were felled and the rude frame of a house reared; when oaks were cut down their branches shaped a vessel's hull, and pines dragged from the near hillsides became her masts. How a stray Indian must have wondered what all this meant and questioned how the coming of a white-winged bird could have effected this change in his landscape!

Door Latches, Bolan House

Seven sons and a daughter were born in this home. Glimpses of the family life, as the years rolled on, show us that in spite of labor there was time for meditation, learning and pleasure. Books still are preserved from the household; religious, school and music books tell us how spare minutes were occupied.

As soon as a son became of age he shipped as a sailor; his home letters were full of thought and consideration for the welfare of parents; a part of his earnings were sent home and his interest in younger brothers and the sister was not lessened. The father's counsel was "never expose yourself unnecessarily but always do your duty;" and the boy was always "your respectful and obedient son."

There was time to help at the houseraising of a neighbor and to join in the festivities that followed; to sip a glass of wine at a wedding, take a friendly cup of afternoon tea or to join a "Christmas frolic" at Colson's.

In later years the family moved to the village and Captain Kempton traded in a store at the Ferryway.

One may visit the Point to-day; find the site of the cabin; the few logs that remained of the wharf but the descendants of this family are scattered in the States.

Just north of the twin oaks at the cemetery one may find a tombstone with this inscription.

In memory of

Capt.

Timothy Lombard

who died at Sea Jan. 22 1804.

Aged 42 years

Anna Lombard his wife

who died March 9 1835

Aged 75 years.

Captain Lombard was a native of Truro, Massachusetts and his wife Anna Collins came from the same town. In 1799 he was a resident of Orrington, buying and selling land at Frankfort. By 1803 he had acquired about three hundred acres and had come to live just north of Judge Goodwin. He was master of the American brig Ranger, a packet and trader. After his death his wife lived at the homestead. Of their many daughters. Thankful Lydia, Nancy, Charlotte, Betsey and Joama, a brother sailor remarked that there was "a lot of them Lombard girls and they married every one in town." There was some truth in this statement when we realize how many of the villagers can claim the Lombard girls as ancestors.

One of the daughters married John Bolan who bought the place and it is now in that family. The low weather-stained walls of the house peer up over the trees at river travelers; and not the least of its attractions are the quaint door latches, many of which are hand made; and which admit us to the hundredyear-old house whose owners appreciate the value of carved mantels, hand-cut wainscoting and other finish that meant hours and hours of skilled labor.

One of the oldest houses in town is standing on the "Tommy Johnson place" which for a century and more remained in the hands of that family. Its original owner, Captain Miller Johnston was of Scotch descent. The name brings to our mind an early colonial governor, a noted general and a little town in Scotland. Captain Johnston came to Frankfort from Nova Scotia about 1789. We know very little of him personally but there are memories of the home and family which interest us. We do know that in his travels he had become a Mason at Newburyport, Massachusetts, in 1776.

Like many of his fellows, as he sailed up the river he liked the location and determined upon it as a home. According to custom a log hut was his first shelter. A landing at the shore was constructed; and a house raised later. The land was improved and an orchard set out. The front door facing the east and the river remind us that the lane which later became a country road, then ran on the river side of the house instead of along the present highway. Probably the original main road can be traced by the old houses which open their doors to the river.

The house was large and well built. Overlooking the river on the north was the sitting-room; this was elaborately finished with scroll and grooved work. Its fireplace seemed enormous to a granddaughter who recalls that she could "sit on a cricket" and be protected in its sheltering sides. On the southern side was the parlor — no one can tell of that because, like all parlors, its curtains were drawn and the doors closed except on state occasions.

The family room, the kitchen, occupied the whole western side of the house and was supplemented by a winter kitchen and the buttery. Its enormous fireplace and the brick oven had all necessary appointments.

Captain Johnston enlisted in the War of 1812 and was at the Battle of Hampden. His fellow townsman, Tobias Oakman, was shot at his side as they were going over a stone wall.

From this enlistment Captain Johnston received Western land, which with the homestead passed into the hands of his only son, Thomas Johnston. Deacon Tommy Johnson and his wife were among the charter members of the present Congregational church. Mr. Johnston was an austere man but greatly respected, and to his wife always fell the duty of making the communion wine.

Their home is remembered by the young people of that day — there was a good orchard; at the shore were the tallest oaks, and a fine swing was suspended there which at high tide swung far out over the river. Altho Ephraim Grant is always hailed as captain, yet his life and influence as a landsman are felt more in the town.

A native of Berwick, Maine, he married Abigail Thurrell, July 4, 1779. With two brothers Adam and William with their families, Ephraim sailed for the Penobscot country — at just what date is unknown. A deed of 1777 says that "Ephraim Grant of Wheelersboro in Penobscot yeoman" sold part of a sawmill. The lumbering and milling advantages drew them here.

Of the two brothers, one settled in the woods a couple of miles inland and traveled to town by spotted trees — where he often preached in Sampson's barn. A few now living remember listening in their youth to the exhortations of Elder Adam Grant. William settled on the west side of Marsh Stream where he built a sawmill four miles inland. His fame and name are not forgotten and many recall stories of the lame old man who was an expert trapper; for the valley of that stream was rich in game and afforded a livelihood to many who hunted the bear, deer and fox.

A log house which had been put up in 1776 became the temporary home of Ephraim. He owned a small vessel, the Mamy Grant. To-day the Post Office, High Head, Chick Common and Ferry Street all lie within the hundred acre lot of his purchase in 1796. He built his frame house just south of meeting house hill.

Material for the frame came from up river; the three brothers went to "Mill Crick," (South Orrington) for Norway pines which were rafted down the river. As they were landed each timber was charred a little; that is, a log was held up about a foot and a half from the ground. The hewings strewn under it as kindlings were set on fire. The Grant barn which is the oldest building in town is now standing at John Carleton's where it was moved in 1854 and its cedar timbers are as sound to-day as when it was built. The nails used were made by the blacksmith's hand.

The family of six children increased to ten. Father and sons converted the wild land into a thrifty farm with hay fields and an orchard. The two yokes of oxen were pressed into service in clearing other lands, hauling wood and ploughing.

On this hilltop town meetings were held "to choose new Officers for Training" or to "see about a minister."

"Feb. 6, 1797, Town meeting at Captain Grant's for the purpose of choosing Federal Representation and doing something about a minister we universally voted for J. Parker for Rep. and voted to give ten dollars to Enoch Mudge, a Methodist preacher as a present towd defraying his traveling expenses."

It is related that in 1812 a captain of the ship Monmouth, who had met with an accident at Castine, unable to proceed with his soldiers was given shelter at Captain Grant's. The English were on the lookout for him, but learning of their approach. Captain Grant shouldered his guest and hid him in the vale in the Sampson pasture where a bed had been prepared for the sick man, who finally escaped and reached his home.

Then Cap'n Grant took his family and journeyed to the Kennebeck. The road to Kennebeck was over Chick Common, thro Goshen, Monroe and Dixmont. When we are told that they returned in winter, making their way on snow shoes and hauling provisions on a sled, we can imagine some of the difficulties of their journey.

In their absence a privateer had anchored in the river, British soldiers had used their home as barracks and when departing had appropriated hay and provisions to take to Castine.

Mr. and Mrs. Grant passed the later years of their life with a son and lived to know that 55 grandchildren "might rise up and call them blessed."

The Giles Memorial of the Sampsons and other families in Plymouth, Massachusetts says that Enoch Sampson was born there March 18, 1758, a son of Stephen, one of six brothers and two sisters.

Captain Sampson came to Buckstown about 1790, then two years later crossed the river to Frankfort. By 1797 he had bought about 900 acres in the settlement, had built a wharf, a house, barn and store where he traded.

He had been a seaman for nearly a year on the armed brig Hazard. This vessel was fitted out in 1777 by the State of Massachusetts and had taken several prizes among them the ship Live Oak.

Of Captain Sampson's sons — one was a town clerk for many years, a captain of the militia company and "a gentleman held in high degree." And Mrs. Sampson's seven daughters are remembered as an "ornament to the community."

One of the most admired views along our Penobscot is that of the Camden Hills. To Frankforters these should have a special interest, personal as weW as artistic. For Mt. Batty, one of the elevations, is more often called by the older people of that town McGlathry's Mountain because its former owner was William McGlathry — who later became a prominent man in Frankfort.

Captain William McGlathry was of Scotch-Irish descent, born in Belfast, Ireland, in 1750. In his boyhood his parents moved to Bristol, Maine. Captain McGlathry and his wife settled in Camden where he was a selectman for some years. Paul Coffin, the Maine Missionary, was entertained at their home and says in his journal "Square McG. treated me with true and simple politeness and hospitality."

He moved to Frankfort and in 1799 built the large square-roofed house which is still remembered by many. It was at the southern end of the village and from its eminence under the elms the inmates could see the British vessels as they went up the river or cast anchor at night-fall waiting to go to the towns above us. Around the large chimney, the finish formed boxes, which could be used as places of concealment at the approach of the enemy. Of the family, a daughter and five sons, Uncle Charlie, a good-natured old man and very moderate in his ways was the last to pass away.

For some years this family had the distinction of owning the one riding carriage in town — this was a two-wheeled chaise which not only did service for the family but for the neighbors as well. A young doctor "lent Esq. McG. my mare to go to Hampden in a chaise for which I am to have his chaise when I want it." One man told me "The first show I ever went to when a young boy was a white bear in a show tent in McGlathry's yard."

During the Revolution Captain McGlathry was sailing a vessel which was captured by a privateer. Three men were put on board to take the prize to Halifax. The captain had been manacled and put on the quarter deck. Seeking some means of escape, he knocked the bung from the water barrel. A crew without fresh water, and ignorant of the coast needed a pilot to take them somewhere for water. The ship's captain was the only one conversant with the coast. He steered her for the nearest port, Machias, whose citizens seized the vessel and its captors became the captured and prisoners of war. Captain McGlathry was allowed to sail for home and safety.

Aside from these recollections the sum of all that is remembered about the "old Square" is that he was always a gentleman.

Ebeneezer Blaisdell, a native of Rhode Island, was a soldier under General Waldo at Fort Pownall and helped in its construction. In his trips up and down the river he had become acquainted with the country and later settled and built a home here.

Some years before his death he divided his property among his ten children giving to Ebeneezer Jr. the homestead. The old house, now 122 years old is the oldest house in town and is still in the family; here yearly the sons of E. Ferrin Blaisdell return, gladly welcomed by old friends and neighbors as the "Blaisdell boys."

Other captains are James Bolan, Jonathan Merrill, Henry and William Mansfield, Amos and James Sproul, Tobias Thompson, Sewell and Isaiah Larabee; the Riches, Nehemiah, John and Nathaniel; a long list of Atwoods, Joshua, Henry, John, Thomas and Nathaniel.

The early packet trade between this and Massachusetts towns, bringing supplies, carrying lumber or perhaps accommodating a few passengers gradually developed into what in later years is known as coasting trade. To-day the term is applied to trade between our port and any on the Atlantic coast of the United States. Many of these crafts have been built here, manned by home sailors and owned by landsmen in the town.

It sometimes seems as if captains "were born not made" when we read of these experiences.

Years ago when the cabin boy and cook on his father's vessel was asked if he could sail a vessel from Rockland to Stockton the answer was "yes." The boy was twelve, his brother of eight acted as mate and probably no man has ever been prouder returning from a rough voyage than those two little chaps when they had steered the Ceylon safely into Stockton harbor. Sailing papers he had none but from that day there could be no question to his title. To-day no part of coastwise waters is unknown to him, he has owned a long list of vessels and now when he has retired, can look back over a life of faithful service, free from accidents and always attended by good luck.

Thro two decades another sailor can recount his experience.

As cabin boy he went to South America. As mate on a vessel that carried out the first governor of Liberia to Sierra Leone he took his first African trip. A testament presented by this governor is treasured as a memento. As sailing master he went to Cape Verde on the Amelia; from there returning to Baltimore with the first oranges that were ever shipped to the United States from that locality. Thirty voyages to the West Indies, many times to Europe and the Mediterranean ports, and his last voyage to Leith, Scotland, the home of his fathers complete the story:

"Home from the Indies and home from the ocean,
  Heroes and soldiers we all shall come home;
  Honored and old and all gaily apparelled.
  Here we shall meet and remember the past."

VII - Highways and Byways

If it is true that all roads lead to Rome, then in the early times our Rome must have been the river; for the settlers of old Frankfort departed from the usual New England custom of laying out villages, placing a meeting house on a green, building the town around it and running all roads thereto or therefrom. They set each house on a hill overlooking the water and for a time the river was a sufficient highway. A path through the woods, traveled by snowshoe in winter, might serve them for an occasional visit to a neighbor's — a mile away. In summer the Indian trail might guide them. But home building and home cares left little time for such intercourse.

Then too in the woods were stragglers more dreaded than the Indian whom they cared not to meet; bears were plenty and it was not unusual to see one trotting past the door; mothers did not allow their children to go far, fearing the wild creatures would get them. One small boy returning from the store with a spool of thread was overtaken by a big fellow puffing along behind him. The frightened child ran for home, bruin ran too but in another direction. Needless to say, no more errands took that lad from home.

Probably the first public way ran to the river. Coulliard's ferry landing was on a point just off High Head, and around the shore to the right the passengers wore a path straight over the hill, thro the woods and into the country. In time this became a bridle road, the ferryway, and by 1804 had been laid out as a "road understood to be three rods wide" and is now Ferry Street. It crossed a road which ran from Belfast to Hampden and it figures in deeds as the "road that goes from Penobscot river towards Kennebeck," and was of some importance in 1792 as the Goshen road.

Two brothers, Joshua and Kenney Coulliard dwelt on either side of the river and tended the ferry. Probably it was no easy task in winter, when the river ran full of floating ice, to manage a dugout, especially if an animal was to be towed behind. The price of conveyance differed, but at one time it was twelve cents one way and ten cents the other.

As Castine was the county seat and chief trade center for the region, anyone who wished to go there must be ferried to Buckstown making the rest of the way on foot or on horseback. From inland came any who had business at Castine Court, while men in public office who consulted with Judge Goodwin on plantation affairs, Indian affairs and on other matters, must ferry here.

Prisoners from hereabouts must be taken to the capital for trial and punishment. We have the following picture of one unfortunate just before his departure.

"I have just come from M—'s in melancholy mood enough. When I went in I found a man there advanced in years indifferently clad, whom M— had taken for debt and was Conducting to Castine Gaol. Yet in these embarrassing circumstances he was playing on the violin and exercising his stiff shoes on the floor in attempts to dance — highly to the merriment of those present."

There is a story that three deserters from the British army at Castine escaped as far as this ferry. Then they were betrayed to their pursuers, taken back down river, and were shot kneeling on their coffins.

Jesse Lee, the founder of Methodism in this province came to Frankfort in 1793. Before this his eloquence had gathered 3000 people on Boston Common. He then started to spread the gospel thro the wilderness — journeying on horseback. His saddle bags contained Bible, hymn book and any necessary clothing. It was a long trip from the Kennebec to Thomaston, crossing the Penobscot to Castine, then up the eastern side of the river where he recrossed to Frankfort. He was gladly received; the people offered to hire him, desiring him to settle among them. But his journal says "it had no weight for I am no hireling" and he returned to Boston by the way of Kennebec.

The ferrymen always command our respect, we are always so dependent upon their judgment for our comings and goings, and whether they live on this side or the other they are always ours. To Mr. James Curtis who for fifty years has plied the oars back and forth over this water we may pay a tribute from our Maine poet.

"Honor and reverence and the good repute —
That follows faithful service as its fruit
Be unto him who living we salute."

He was always ready to respond to the bell which swung from its high post at the foot of the hill and no captain of an ocean liner had more the confidence of his passengers than he had. Authority on all weather, he knew winds, tides and fogs, and no matter how dark the night or how rough the river, we knew that with him we should reach the other side.

The stretch of woods now known as Chick Common lies up over the hill on either side of the old Goshen road. Altho we had no church green this served as a common or gathering-place. To it ran Cowpath Lane where the village cattle went to graze. One settler "let his mare run on the common and found it nearly as good as the neighboring pastures." But one day she was needed for a professional call and was not to be found.

For the last generation it has been a favorite picnic ground. Hemlocks, pines and birches grew there while oaks and many large beeches made it a resort for family parties in the nutting season. They used to take sheets and spread them on the ground. The boys climbed the trees to shake the big branches while the girls gathered the nuts into bags; and before going home perhaps each one cut his name in the silvery bark high up as he could reach. If we walk thro the avenue of the common now we see but few of the big trees, some even yet showing the marks of picnic times. — And from many stumps spring the fresh green twigs of new trees, while near by are fallen trunks whose old leaves, now transparent parchment, still cling to the branches.

The first record of road making which I found was in Judge Goodwin's diary. In 1792 he mentions "working on the road." The felling of trees, digging out roots and stumps must have been work indeed. In the fall of 1794 he "began to work on the County Road and laid the string pieces of a bridge back of Bolan's." This bridge was covered the following December.

Previously there had been rough ways, sufficient for hauling lumber and firewood. The ox was used as beast of burden. A vehicle for taking lumber to market after the snow had gone was called a car. This was made of two poles with rungs like a ladder. One end dragged on the ground and the forward end was left open for the horse; the poles, entering rings in the harness, were fastened there by pins. The horse collar was of twisted hay. This harness often led to dissension among drivers. The horses, while waiting for their masters to trade, would secure a meal from one another's collars.

The county road lay between Hampden and Belfast. Each of these towns were small settlements then. Several rods back from it lay the "old road" to the Marsh which was probably used for wood hauling. This was discontinued later.

At the opening of the century, sleighs and wheeled vehicles were in use. On the 22d of February, 1800, Doctor Goodwin...
"went up to Hampden with Captain Sampson in his sleigh and we walked in procession from Captain Wheelers' to the meeting house, the Company of Artillery and the free masons and military officers, judicial officers. Town officers strangers and Citizens where the Rev. Enoch Mudge addressed the throne of Grace, several pieces of music an ode composed by Mrs. Mudge and a very pertinent address to the free masons and the rest of the assembly on the sublime Nature of our departed friend Father and Brother General George Washington — the same was very solemn."

Town meetings have been held on the public highway. We know of one in the plantation which was held on a lumber pile near the cross roads and it was voted that "no person should be permitted to play at Ball, Quoits, Ninepins, or any other game in highways or town ways, under penalty of two Dollars each for Each offense."

At the present time a Norway pine stands alone in a field near the Bolan bridge and is known as the Bacon tree. After the cocoa episode of 1779 when the British fleet had departed down river, a sloop, under a flag of truce, returned to the village demanding the cocoa. Some of it had been taken on board when Lieutenant Morse discovered arms on her. He threw the cocoa overboard, set fire to the sloop, took her crew prisoners and departed. Our people became so alarmed, fearing a return of the British, that many fled to the country, many burned their household goods or buried silver in the gardens. But this old Pine did good service by concealing within its thick foliage the valuables of Judge Goodwin — his silver and supply of hams. He desired that this tree be preserved and cared for.

Along this County Road traveled so many different people and on such different errands.

Now it is a party of ladies and gentlemen who are making their way on horseback to Mount Misery. They decide that it deserves a better name and one of the number climbs a tree, breaking a bottle and gives it the name of Mount Waldo.

Now it is a group of villagers, in 1814, hastening to Beale Mountain to watch the coming of the enemy. Three ships come in sight, their troops all on deck, in gay uniform. They were impressed when, six days later on the return from the Hampden battle, these same troops appeared and demanded provision and cattle. A strange sight indeed to see Redcoats and gaily dressed Germans in green jackets and high hats on this quiet highway.

The Bacon Tree

And again our own soldiers paced it as they went to Captain Grant's for training or marched to and from that same battle.

Like Rome of old we have our seven hills. At North Frankfort is the long Sabine hill; at the southern end of town, Guide Board hill whose mile post directs us to Belfast or out past the site of gypsy camps, past the old watering trough to Mouseville and Monroe; between them lie Sproul's, Thayer's, Cushing's and Shaw's hills. Last but by no means least there is Christian Hill so named, I am told, because the families there were so united and lived in such a friendly way.

In the dark days of Civil War, now and then at nightfall a footsore traveler is seen making his way along the highroad and seeking the big house on Cushing's hill because it was an underground station and he could spend a comfortable night, and in the morning be set on his way to Bangor. From thence he could reach the border.

Across on the opposite hill free hospitality was dispensed. An invitation to a wedding at Square Shaw's is dated "Jackson Hill 12 o'clock at night, Apr. 18, 1829" and shows the political inclinations of its owner. A grand ball was given here at the inauguration of the seventh president. Shaw's hill or the Lebanon road as it is now called is an extension of Commercial street which had been laid out or swamped from the county road to the river.

Down town the land bounded by Main, Marine, Mechanic and Holmes streets is known as The Square. The last three streets probably were laid out soon after 1841 when the steam mill was running. The large white house at the corner of Mechanic and Holmes streets was built for a mill boarding house. For many years it was vacant and was supposed to be haunted. A street runs diagonally across the square. A plan had been on foot to build a church on the site of the present Catholic Church. The big house now owned by Mrs. Anne Bowden, was designed for a parsonage, and the name Parsonage street was given to the thoroughfare. A disagreement arose among the promoters of the religious society and the house was sold. At one time it accommodated five families, three of them French; and later, a Quaker family lived there.

Down over the hill below Mechanic street is a hollow familiarly known as the Holler. Here before 1850 settled many Irish families who had come to work in the mill. The names Kelley, Morrisey, McDermott, McDonough, McCormack, Mogan, Lathlin, and Foley are familiar.

Whig street extends from Mr. Frank Haley's store to Carleton's corner and on to Cole's corner. An enclosed triangle is formed where it crosses the old Goshen road in the center of which for many years stood an oak. At one time it was proposed to make a park of this land and once it was mentioned as a site for the soldier's monument. The men most influential in the laying out of this street were whigs, hence its name.

A newspaper of 1855 has the following in its editorial. "We need an organized effort to improve our village." It recommends "an extension of Mechanic street to Main; that Oak street be extended along the shore till it connects with Water street at the ferry. This would open up a number of building and wharf lots for market." It also states that the "destruction of old oak groves and murmuring pines which graced the rear of our village have nearly or quite disappeared," and "the town is barren of ornamental trees in foliage except where private enterprise has embellished private streets and residences."

The rows of elm trees which now ornament the county road or the Main street did not simply happen there, but are due to the enterprise of six or seven young men of the town. Only two of these men, Benjamin Atwood and Bradford Dean are living, and one of them says: "I never visit my old home without feeling proud of this day's work about which we thought so little when we were doing it."

As we were on two stage lines — the Belfast and Bangor route and the one to Hallowel and Boston — there were many taverns along the road. Their keepers were men of consequence in the community, for in those days landlords must be men recommended by town officers. To their care travelers must entrust themselves and their valuables often.

The old Chick House was formerly an inn and was built in 1807 by a Mr. Martin. He built far beyond his means, the neighbors say, and they called it Martin's Folly. It was originally a hip-roofed house, but when it was repaired in 1857, was changed. Weird tales were told to children, that it was a haunted house. It contained a large dance hall and at one gathering when a ball was given, a British soldier attempted to enter; he was shot on the stairs. After that the slumber of many a guest was disturbed by strange and unusual sounds which were supposed to be the footsteps of this soldier who, in his uniform, was pacing the floor by night. Later a Mr. Rowe was landlord. Again dances were held in the hall and the country people enjoyed eight hand reels. Journey to Boston, etc., to the strains of Jack Douglas's fiddle and went home the next forenoon. The following rhyme shows how Mr. Rowe stood with the traveling public.

"The Bangor House is a house of fame
The Hampden House is also the same
The Frankfort House is very well
But they can't hold a candle to Rowe's hotel."

The Kelley homestead was also a tavern, built in 1802 by a Mr. Cox. While a chimney was being repaired in recent years, the mason found a letter hidden there which was addressed to a British officer in Castine from one in Frankfort.

Another public house was the one now occupied by Caleb R. Lougee. It was kept by Aaron Holbrook. Bar-room and hall were on either side of the entry and many entertainments were held in the latter, among them was an exhibition of wax works, one of the figures being Lady Helen Mar.

The Little tavern, now the home of Mrs. John Sproul, which was erected about 1814, is not far from this. Three large trees stood in front of it. Between them and the door was a driveway and from the largest oak was suspended a sign which creaked as it swung in the wind.

A tavern was kept, on the Goshen road near the Blaisdell farm, by a Scotchman, John Spearing. This was a stage stand where post horses were changed, and a house for the accommodation of teamsters. This house had for many years one guest known to many as a forgotten hero, Hatevil Colson, who in his younger days had been an extensive land owner, yeoman his deed is signed.

Disappointment in love had made him a wanderer thro the country, a tramp. He roamed over the state, cared for by anyone at whose door he sought shelter, always a welcome visitor; yet good-natured Hate regarded this tavern as his home. He was always ready to render a good turn, and as often his keen wit played some wild prank wherever his fancy led him.

He appeared at Castine during its occupation by the British and asked one of the generals if he had ever seen a Yankee humming bird. The gentleman said that he had not, so Hate promised to get one, adding that they were fine singers. He soon came back with a hornet's nest, the opening of which had been stopped up. The general was informed that if he wished to hear them sing he must put the nest in a closed room with even the keyhole sealed. This was done according to orders; captain and officers shut themselves into the vessel's cabin — and the birds did begin to sing. Of course they were badly stung. The country was scoured for the culprit but Hate had fled to the woods.

During one January thaw some children were playing near the main road and Hate came along with a pair of new shoes. Taking his knife he cut a piece from each toe and heel, put them on and started to walk thro the slush and melting snow. When the curious children asked why he did it, he said: "Why, to let the water run out when it runs in, of course."

In the ell chamber at the tavern were several straw beds. Also boxes of grain, some oats, and peas were stored. One day Hate sewed all of them, about forty bushels, into the straw ticks and ran away. The landlord's thirteen children were kept from mischief for some time sorting out the mixture. He came back not long after and when Mrs. Spearing asked him why he did it, he said: "Now, now, don't you worry about that, we'll have the garden of Eden and it will be a beautiful spot."

Perhaps he was irresponsible, but we may also remember his good deeds; when he made his way to Belfast to warn the inhabitants of the coming of the British and saved their cattle; or of his long tramp to Hampden to warn the farmers to be on the look out. The last year of his life he was "bid off" to a new home where he died in June 1821, and the last rite his landlord could perform for him was to plant a tree on his grave.

Among other taverns was the big house at the foot of ferry hill, a haunt of sailors and seamen; the Kemptons kept a hotel at the top of the same hill. At the lower village was the old Frankfort house kept by Major Hersey. At its burning the bucket brigade exhausted the big brook at the foot of Whig street.

The Commercial house was built in 1833 or 34; the bricks were of home production from the clay bank at the foot of Commercial street. Its old registers bear many interesting names and the pages are elaborately decorated with announcements of shows to appear at Clark's hall. The grand jubilee and ball at the incorporation of the town of Winterport, April 30, 1860 was held in it. In front of the house hung a transparency bearing "Winterport, 1860." "All was life and animation within" says the paper, "where the rooms were filled with a happy crowd enjoying themselves in social conversation. At twelve o'clock supper was served, which was a credit to mine host Johnson...who ever enjoyed a reputation second to no landlord for many miles around."

Four and eight horse concord coaches stopped at this hotel daily en route to Black's corner. Here and at Black's comer were the relays of horses. The coaches accommodated nine and twelve passengers during the Aroostook war and the days of speculation and there was plenty to do. The postal service was by stage and in '49 and '50 the arrival of California mail was announced by the display of an American flag in front of the post office. In those years people would have to stay here two and three days waiting to take the boat, so hotels flourished. But with the installation of telegraph, guests became fewer, business declined. With the coming of steam the stage coach and post chaise gradually disappeared.

VIII - The Settlers and Their Homes

The demands which a new country made upon its pioneers were much greater than those which settlers at a later date were called upon to meet. They endured privation and hardship which served to develop consciences keen to do the right and characters strong and vigorous. From their lives comes an influence to us thro the years. There were many men and women who gave the best of themselves to family, to neighbors and to their country, but of whose everyday lives but few facts are preserved; yet at the sound of their names, some memory is revived, some noble influence is felt. Truly this is a lasting remembrance and more enduring than any written word. They will never be truly forgotten.

There were farmers, John Hegan, William Sullivan, Paul Downes, Benjamin Stubbs, John Carleton and Moses Littlefield; — who plowed and sowed and reaped, whose days were uneventful. Yet when the country needed their service, they shouldered guns and responded to her call as quickly as did the minute men of Lexington.

Altho these settlers had come to a new country and must endure the discomforts of a Maine winter in rude and unplastered houses, there was little illness among them. There was not time for it. So for a few years there was no physician nearer than Fort Point until Doctor Goodwin came.

In the disastrous defeat of the Penobscot expedition in July 1779, when the vessels of the American fleet had been scattered up river, the flag ship Warren was run ashore by her crew just off Oak Point. Some of her timbers may still be found in the mud at the December tides; a few pieces have been recovered and kept as relics, in the town and in the museum at Plymouth. To prevent capture by the British, the crew set fire to her, while they took to the woods and made their way home by land.

It may not be commonly known that the hero of that famous midnight ride to Lexington once camped not far from our borders. For it was in this same expedition that Colonel Paul Revere was in command of the ordnance; and at the dispersal of the fleet at Castine he was ordered to follow his general, Peleg Wadsworth up river. In his diary he says: "I went up as far as Grant's mills where I landed to wait for my boat — went a mile into the woods and camped for night, set off then for Kennebec." For this seeming insubordination he was reprimanded and three years passed before he was vindicated.

The surgeon's mate on the Warren was Francis LeBaron Goodwin, who at this time obtained some knowledge of the country and, in after years, made a permanent home a half mile below the scene of the disaster.

Francis LeBaron Goodwin, the sixth son of Lydia LeBaron and Nathaniel Goodwin was born in Plymouth, Sept. 29, 1762. On his mother's side he traced his ancestry back to a "Nameless Nobleman." It was a hundred years before the Penobscot affair that a French privateer, its name now unknown, had been wrecked in Buzzard's bay. The officers and crew were at once made prisoners and started for Boston. On the way there, they were quartered for the night on Plymouth green. The ship's surgeon — Francis LeBaron — thro some slight office which he performed for a sick woman near by, received permission to practice medicine in the colony. The doctor could not speak English, the colonists could not speak French, so John Cotton conversed with him in Latin. He lived many useful years among them and died in the faith of his fathers, the Roman Catholic. It was rumored that he was a Huguenot who had been compelled by his parents to enter a Jesuit college for the priesthood; but that this was not his choice. So he had escaped over the monastery wall and found refuge on the ship. Miss Austin made him the hero of her popular novel. The Nameless Nobleman. A visit to Plymouth town may easily find his tombstone on the crest of burial hill.

"Here Lyes Ye Body
of Mr. Francis LeBaron
Physician who
Departed this life
Aug. Ye 8— 1704.
In Ye 36 year
of his age."

Of his three sons, one, Lazarus, followed his profession and lived in the colony town, on the site of the Samoset house. Miss Austin has also pictured him and his family in "Dr. LeBaron's Daughters." It was the daughter of this Doctor Lazarus who became the mother of our Doctor Goodwin.

Nathaniel Goodwin had accumulated a good estate, many houses and lands; he did considerable shipping, owned several vessels and a wharfage. So that his son must have become familiar with the sea; and must have acquired much knowledge from the sailors who frequented his father's warehouse and the tavern house in Leyden street. His birth place is still standing nearly opposite Pilgrim Hall and is known now as the "Bacon house."

The town school was kept by Alexander Scannell and he may have attended this, but it is more probable that he obtained his early education at a private school, kept by Peleg Wadsworth, the grandfather of Henry Wadsworth Longfellow.

Doctor Lazarus LeBaron died in 1773 and some of his medical library may have fallen to his grandson; but it is likely that his medical education was obtained from Dr. William Thomas.

To him, at his father's death in 1771, fell the house in Court street and this was his home till he came to Penobscot. The spirit of unrest was upon him and for a time, instead of following medicine, he was interested in shipping, buying and selling lumber. Then, too, he kept up with affairs of the world, for his diary tells us that

"Apr. 1776 President & Corporation &c of Harvard College conferred the degree of Doctr of Laws on General Washington."

"July 4, 1776 The Grand Continental Congress declared ye 13 United Colonies free and independent States which was received with universal applause thro the continent."

So vitally interested was he that for six years he served as a commissioned officer in the fourteenth, ninth and third Massachusetts regiments. He must have been in the New Jersey campaign and in quarters at West Point; for from Camp New Bridge, in a letter to a brother he deplores the fact that he has heard from home but eight times in an absence of five months. It shows that he suffered the inconveniences of that hard winter when currency was useless and food and clothing scarce.

Sept. 12, 1780.

"Most of the time we have been Cantoned in tents. We generally encamp about a week, long enough to get all things to Writes & then Gen'l Beats which is to strike your tent and march away; at our first Encampment after we left King's ferry which was at Orangetown I was left to take care of the sick of our Division which is commanded by a Gen'l called the Baron of Steuben: there I tarried 3 weeks which time I spent agreeably, then had orders to join * * * while on the march to Hackensack to where our next push will be I cannot inform you. I am not well prepared for winter on account of clothes but am in hopes of getting some from the State, how that will be I cannot say."

In January 1781 he writes from "West Point Huts;" these Huts were the winter quarters of the Continental troops and were in the woods a couple of miles in the rear of the works. He communicates with Major Gamaliel Bradford about the

"purchase of a bed and its furniture which would be of Infinite Service to me as I am destitute — if it would suit you to part with them I will make you ample compensation the first Opportunity that Occurs

Your Very Humble Servant

F. L. G."

At this time he received a letter from his brother, Lazarus, wishing him success in his profession.

"You have, my dear brother, my earnest prayer for your advancement in life, and may you make such proficiency in Surgery as will do Honor to the profession. I would have you pay the greatest attention as you have a fine opportunity to gain experience. I hope to see you return an accomplished Gentleman without the Vices Incident to the Army. It is a school of politeness but it requires Judgment to avoid the excesses which some of the officers run into, your prudence, I hope, will deter you from them.

Lazarus."

He did enjoy the intercourse of army life and was one of the original members of the Society of Cincinnati, that fraternity which was formed to cherish the friendships made in those trying days of the Revolution. Dr. Goodwin refers to it later in his journal.

At the close of the war, he came home and turned his attention to making money — this time with some incentive. Not far from the Court street cottage was the house of Chandler Robbins, pastor of the first church of Plymouth. As Mr. Robbins was a proficient French scholar, had been at Yale, Dartmouth and the University of Edinburgh, a visitor to his home must have imbibed these influences. The young doctor had become a frequent visitor to the house, and finally paid court to the divine's daughter; his diary relates the sequel —

"Oct. 12. 1786. This Day was Determined a matter of great consequence."

"Oct. 18, 1786. This day Esq. Spooner published our Intentions to the Congregation. Parson Sampson of Plimpton preached."

"June 28, 1787. Married to Miss Jenny Robbins.

Went to housekeeping next day."

After a couple of years of practice in Plymouth, Doctor Goodwin came to Frankfort with John Kempton to look up a farm. He finally purchased one of Hatevil Colson — "50 acres in consideration of three good cows." The men lived on Oak Point for two months, returned to Plymouth, and the following spring Mr. Goodwin came back to build a house. The records of its construction show some of the trials which beset a pioneer.

1790 June Ye 22 Mr. Lane came to work to frame and set up my house for 9 Bush Com or the Value of it. My finding him & one man while they are to work on it."

July 1 All hands went over to Raize my house but night came on & we could not get ready. Next morning all came again & put it up before 12 o'clock."

"...July 14 I went to Marsh Bay Mills for my Boards."

"...17 Hagan halld Boards up to the frame this afternoon."

"1790 Aug. 16 Peter Holmes was coming which he did in the afternoon & brought my Bricks & Lime."

21 Went up River to Wheelers Mills & purchased 2 M Boards & Rafted them Down to Oak Point 1 o'clock night & the next Monday to my place."

24 Eben Weilding came to work to enclose my house at 1 Bushel Corn pr Day or the value thereof."

"...26 Raised 26 feet x 18 11-2 story high."

..Sept. 12 Mr. Groce a mason & Mr. Gorton came ye 13 to put up my chimneys. My Grain Eyes are 23 inches apart."

..Oct. 1 Mr. Gorton & Mr. Groce came to finish my chimneys & compleated them Saturday noon & went home."

The following month Mr. Goodwin went to Plymouth for the household goods and arrived at Frankfort, December 3.

"Run up to Kempton's Cove in morning and look out my things, soon after I landed and took possession of my new open house it set in a severe snowstorm and cont'd all night and I had hearth laid in my Keeping Room that afternoon and took up my abode and tarried there until ye first of Jan'y then went over to John Kemptons to live the rest of the Winter they was to Cook and wash for me for my Setting the Boys Copies and learning them to Write."

"1791 May ye 6th Sett off from Plymouth with my Family for Penobscot in Capt. Jesse Churchill, the next Monday noon ye 9th Instant Mrs. Leonard on board, Francis sick. Chimney gone and hell to pay. Charles Kempton and myself went Immediately up river after Mr. Gorton and Returned that Night and in two Day he got the foundation up, hearth lay'd etc.

The days that followed were busy ones: the home land must be cleared, ploughed, and crops put in. Then the house must be completed and furnished. In reply to a letter from the anxious mother in Plymouth, Mrs. Goodwin tells of their comforts and says

"We have new merchants moved into the River. I can bye almost anything here that you can in Plymouth but at a much dearer rate." and again, "our

Room is plastered and very warm, don't think there is one warmer in Penobscot, there is but three or four Plastered in the Place."

Other letters assured the mother of how the money came in little by little and of the kindness of the young husband. From the colony various gifts would come — pepper, vinegar, a pot of butter, now and then a book, or perhaps a quilt for little Frank. Family cares had increased. The baby Francis now had brothers and when Dr. Goodwin went to Boston, together with his memorandum of official business, his wife would send one of family needs.

"7 yds Cotton & linen Cloth for children.
Tow cloth for table and toweling,
Castor oyle & Paragorick,
Shoes for Frank and Larra (Lazarus.)
Narrow velvet for Frank's hat."

The life of a doctor was not easy, as there were trips to Hampden, Prospect, thro the country and over the river, and to professional cares were added those of state. He became Justice of Peace and must make out deeds, settle disputes and perform marriages. He became Judge and must attend Court at Castine. He was chosen Representative to the general court at Boston and must go there once or twice a year. It was on one of these trips that he tells us he met his old friends.

"July 4, 1795 Independent Day walked with the Representatives in procession attended by the Boston Independent Compy Artiely Compy and all the free masons to assist in Laying the Corner Stone of the new State House the Governor made a very animated speech I suppose but I did not hear but three words they were very good and after the Ceremony was over I went to Concert Hall and Dined with our Brethren the Society of Cincinnatus had a very agreeable time was exceedingly gratified in seeing my old Continental acquaintances."

Paul Revere assisted at this ceremony as Grand Master of the Masonic order and the governor mentioned is Samuel Adams. It might be interesting to know some of the acquaintances who gathered at this dinner at the brick Inn on Hanover street at which had feasted Sons of Liberty, noted masons, and now this interesting assembly.

Sometimes Mrs. Goodwin would accompany him, and go down to Plymouth for a visit. And to his diary he confides his loneliness.

"Sept. 12 — 1794 end of departure of wife for Plym. This night feel very dull. Wife gone, no children, not even Sanco, nothing but Catts & Crickets."

",.15 Sanco came home."

. . 191 came home quite a lonesome house only the Catt & Kittens to be seen."

"Nov. 2, 1794 No wife come yet—been gone 7 weeks last Fryday—am quite tired of living alone. Ye Take care next time."

Mrs. Goodwin's death occurred just after a return of Mr. Goodwin from Boston, "to the inexpressible grief of all present but more particularly to myself," he says "who never expect to repair the exceeding heavy bereavement of Providence. She was decently & Solemnly Buried near our house. Mr. Mudge here & preached a Funeral Sermon."

If we go to the Goodwin farm to-day, we may follow a path of sweet fern, thro' a tangle of brakes, to a growth of young birches and oaks overlooking the river; and there, under a pine whose needles have half covered the stone we may dimly read this epitaph,

"Sacred
to the memory of
Mrs. Jane P. Goodwin the
virtuous Consort of
Francis LeBaron
Goodwin Esq
Died July 29, 1801
Aged 37 years."

Francis Goodwin passed his last days in public service and came to his death in 1816 by being thrown from a horse. Four sons were born to them; Francis LeBaron, born Dec. 18, 1789; Chandler Robbins, born Feb. 15, 1792, and died in the West Indies July 2, 1817; Lazarus, born March 21,1 796; and William LeBaron, born Apr. 22, 1800. Francis LeBaron Goodwin Jr. remained on the farm and followed his father in holding offices of trust in the town; he was a lieutenant in the state militia in 1822. His son, Chandler Robbins Goodwin was, too, an honored citizen.

Francis LeBaron;
Lazarus LeBaron, — Lydia Bartlett Lydia LeBaron — Nathaniel Goodwin Francis LeBaron Goodwin — Jane Prince Robbins Francis" "Jr. — Hannah B. Dean Chandler Robbins Jr. — Coraline B. Dillingham. Delphina Francis Goodwin — Frank W. Haley Millie C. Haley, Charles M. Haley.

Dr. Peabody remained but a few years and built and occupied the house known as the "Robinson house," now owned by Mr. Daniel Moody. He moved to Levant and Doctor Abbott established himself here.

EDMUND LORD ABBOTT.

"Nurtured in the lap of indulgence from early infancy by the tenderest, best of parents, parents whose every wish has centered in my happiness & every exertion has tendered to promote it — to Berwick will I look as the pole star of my affection."

Thus writes a young man who after long and careful deliberation has determined upon Frankfort as a good place in which to begin his life as a physician; he writes at the close of the first day of his practice; (May 24, 1804). This may account for the bit of longing and of homesickness which are evident.

Edmund Abbott was the only child of Daniel Abbott and Abigail Lord of Berwick, Maine. He was a graduate of Harvard Medical School.

From the early surroundings, of which he has given us an idea, it must have taken some courage to leave them, to make his own way in the world.

Upon arriving at Frankfort, he found another young doctor ahead of him — Dr. Green: this was the cause of much worry, as the undertaking of a new case or the loss of an old one was of vital importance to each.

The chief illness in the place was bilious fever: the common remedies were salts of myrrh, vinegar and indian meal poultices: "blooding" was often resorted to. A young practitioner's stock in trade consisted of a few books, and his vials of medicine could all be stored in saddlebags still in the attic at Abbott place.

Doctor Abbott's journal for his first year contains many pages, which show his anxiety about the approval of one settler or another; about whether or not Frankfort had been a wise choice. Then too the question of money troubled him; patients were slow to pay — and many did not pay at all. So he pieced out a living in various ways, buying hay, making out tax bills and even by teaching school. In making a decision about accepting the latter position he says, "I believe I must, altho I have a violent aversion to it." During the time which he did teach we find these comments,

"Considerably interrupted by my business,"

"Mac complained that I was too late in the morning at school (patients)."

However, the sky cleared and money began to come in; he bought land. Then as he had become tired of boarding he decided to have a home; purchased a lot of Ephraim Grant, cleared away a few trees, got out lumber on the spot and put up a two-story house. As most of the houses at that time were one story, this high building was called the "lighthouse." The southern half of the Abbot house, as it stands to-day was the original structure.

He had accumulated enough so that marriage was possible. A Miss Alice Ware, a daughter of Dr. William Ware of Dighton, Massachusetts, visited now and then her uncle, William Andrews. Doctor Abbott had met her and in 1808 they were married. Altho the little bride could weave and embroider her own wedding gown, she was not versed in the gentle art of housekeeping. However the demands on a country doctor's wife were many, and necessity proved a good teacher. It was not long before she could manage toaster, bakers, skillets and brass kettles as deftly as she had plied the needle. And we can picture her as the inquisitive children gather around while she brushes the coals from the cover of the bake kettle; and they wonder what savory dish will come from its black interior — steaming baked beans, or bread or — the longed-for cookies.

At nightfall when the pine logs lay across the andirons, she sits sewing, waiting for the return of her husband, who has been on a long ride thro the woods. Then she hears the sound of horse's hoofs coming nearer, and sees the dim light, thro the isinglass sides of the old square lantern. She meets him at the door with the candle of her own making. From the capacious saddle bags perhaps, he brings a gift — sent by some grateful patient. They talk over the calls and the patients, while she sits, with a foot on the little wooden cradle; a cradle now treasured at Abbott place, as it has rocked three generations. With it are stored there many of the old furnishings.

A Wedding Gown; Hand Woven, Hand Embroidered, Hand Made

Doctor Abbott died in 1853, July 18, having practiced in Frankfort for fifty-one years. His son, Dr. Charles Abbott succeeded him here for thirty years. A grandson, Edmund Abbott, is now a practicing physician in Providence, Rhode Island.

Daniel Abbott — Abigail Lord
Berwick, Me.   Berwick
Dr. Edmund Abbott — Alice Ware
Frankfort, Me.   Dighton, Mass.
Dr. Charles Abbott — Harriet C. Newell Chick
Winterport, Me.   Winterport, Me.
Dr. Edmund Abbott — Charlotte Moore
Providence, R. I.   Providence, R. I.

SIMEON SABINE.

A name which is probably unfamiliar, if not quite unknown to the younger generation, is that of Simeon Sabine, a resident of North Frankfort.

Every teamster on his way from Bangor to Belfast, must in one place at least be kind to his horses; on the long hill which runs south from the Cove. A resting-place is invariably just above the little yellow house which nestles by the roadside and whose windows peer out at passers-by thro a hedge of lilacs.

Not much of the owner's family history is preserved, except that he was born in Attleborough, Massachusetts, Aug. 14, 1773. It was known that he owned a plantation in the South which he visited now and then, and he was called by his northern friends a "niggerdriver" — slaveowner.

Simeon Sabine was interesting to his neighbors because they knew so little of his early life; he was loved by them because — he was a "father to everybody" as one, who had received a kindness at his hand, has said.

He had married Polly Billings of Sharon, Mass., and moved to the Cove where he built the little house. At the waterside near the bridge he built a store where he traded and kept the post office.

The Sabines were followers of Universalism — in those days a hated belief — yet they attended the Orthodox church in the village, and Mr. Sabine wrote for religious papers. In spite of creed he was consulted by all the country-side on personal matters and on business affairs. While many a sick one watched for the footsteps of the kind little white-turbaned woman who ministered to their needs; or were gladdened by gifts and messages dispensed by Mr. Sabine, who always said "This from the good woman." One man, now old, recalls how when his eleven brothers and sisters were ill with the measles, Mr. Sabine came up over the long hill and across the snow on hands and knees to bring them a bushel of crackers.

Mr. Sabine, with Benjamin Shaw and General Jedediah Herrick, served on the County Commission. In the days of Square Shaw's prosperity, days of the Frankfort bank, there were teas and weddings; from letters which passed between the families we may judge that many social hours were spent together. "Should the weather be pleasant we shall expect you and Mr. Sabine with Miss Atwood to-morrow evening and hope you will not disappoint us.

B. S."

"The Marriage of my Daughter will take place this evening and we shall be much pleased to have you attend and shall expect you at Tea at six o'clock.

"B. S."

"Brother Sabine,

I regret that circumstances render it inconvenient for me to partake to-morrow of that hospitality which always flows so spontaneously from your generous noble soul. I shall be with you soon and will endeavor to attend meeting with you probably Sabbath after next. B. S.

Please say to the Gen'l should you see him that I will be up about the trees."

The old white horse, which bore the dignified and stately general thro the country on his trips as surveyor or commissioner, often might be seen tethered at the Sabine door. General Herrick's daughter and Mrs. Sabine were friends and exchanged frequent visits when the latter could be persuaded to spend a day at the fine old mansion at Hampden corner. The manner of their intercourse may be learned from this letter:

"My dear Friend

You will perceive that I am improving for herewith you receive the last papers you lent me before they are actually worn out or become ruined by long possession. I agree with you 'Mrs. Trollop has written many books' but she has not written like a Lady. After these refreshing dewes shall have passed will you not be tempted to come and spend a day with us. We all want to see you & can't you be content to leave your quiet and elegant home for one day. I expect to have some interesting books soon and shall send you whatever I know to be worth your perusal. I am ashamed to be always reminding you of my carelessness but I left a pocket handkerchief at your house, I think upon the table in the dining room, which if you have noticed will you give to father.

With sentiments of unfeigned Love & Respect Your & Mr. Sabine's most humble

Friend Clara C. Herrick."

Mr. and Mrs. Sabine had no children, but adopted a daughter who took the name, Elmira Billings Sabine. She later married Aaron Holbrook of Hampden. In letters to a sister, this daughter has left us two pictures of her parents.

"I wish you could have known her. She has been to me a kind and indulgent mother and most sincerely do I lament the loss of her to whom I have hitherto looked up for counsel and guidance."

A Quiet and Elegant Home in 1829

"I am happily situated here — my adopted father, Mr. Sabin is one of the best of men & I cannot be sufficiently thankful for his kindness and the indulgence with which he treats me. If were his own daughter he could treat me no better & I trust that he will long live to be a father & protector for me."

Mr. Sabine had been considered wealthy, and years after his death, part of the cellar wall was torn out as it was rumored that gold was buried there. When he died in 1839, he left a will, but a seal and signature were lacking which made it necessary to dispose of his household effects at auction. Thus some of the family silver, bearing the initials S. P. S. (Simeon and Polly Sabine), is treasured in a few homes in the town to-day.

After three score years have passed; his reputation — an honest man, always good, always charitable — still lives.

IX - The Settlers and Their Homes (Continued.)

One visiting old Frankfort in the early part of the last century might easily fancy himself in an English shire town, so often would he hear the title of Esquire. But already the New England dialect was developing, and "Square" Merrill, "Square" Jones and "Square" Shaw were familiar appellations. Any Justice of Peace or lawyer was addressed thus; and there were certainly enough of the latter to keep people either in trouble or out of it. John Pike, Philo Washburn and Albert Kelly were early lawyers.

SAMUEL MERRILL

Do you remember some April day when the snow is just beginning to leave the hills and you have gone thro the cemetery and into the ravine back of it? You made your way around the "muck hole," across the brook and climbed the opposite hill, and there uncovered hidden treasures — the trailing arbutus or May flowers in Merrill's woods? Then your way home led thro the field behind the big house where you were treated to a ride on the back of the blind pony which belonged to the Merrill boys.

In early fall, the shortest way home from school was always through their large orchard, whence you emerged with pockets full of Martha stripes or sweet russets.

Samuel Merrill, the original owner of this farm, was born in 1777. He came to Frankfort from Conway, New Hampshire. The land he bought from Mr. Oakman and cut the timbers for the house right where it stands.

Mr. Merrill had a store on the old brick school house lot; was prominent in religious affairs; was clerk of a society which was known as the North West Union Society. He was also Justice of Peace.

His death occurred January 1, 1852, and the farm passed to a son, Chandler Merrill. It is now the home of Albert Merrill, a grandson.

ARCHIBALD JONES

Altho there is no one here to perpetuate the Jones name, yet the family influence is felt among us. Our post-office building which was finished and first occupied in 1823 was for years the family residence. In those days there were green blinds on the house, and over the front door was a latticed frame with seats at either side, while over the frame ran woodbine and honeysuckle. From this door to the street there was a path bordered with old-fashioned flowers. By the roadside and along the garden fence stood a row of rock maple trees. The north side of the house was also shaded by maples.

Behind the house was a dense growth of evergreens, brought by the children of the family from the nearest forest and planted. The trees grew up with the children and soon became much higher than the house, making a beautiful background for it as seen in passing on the river. On the south side of the lot was the fruit and vegetable garden.

Archibald Jones, "Counsellor at Law," was born in Worcester, Massachusetts in 1777 and died at Frankfort, February 9, 1858. He had come to Penobscot in 1802 at about the same time that Mr. Oakman, Dr. Abbott and Benjamin Thompson came. Thinking that he saw in its position, at the head of winter navigation, the possibility of a chief city on the river, he chose to settle in Frankfort. He was admitted to court at Portland in 1806; became attorney for the heirs of the Waldo Patent, as they owned land in this and surrounding counties. He also became active in town affairs.

Mr. Jones was a most upright man, of fine mind and a deep student of all religions.

His marriage was in 1811 to Miss Sally Woodman of New Hampshire. From this union were four children who lived to adult age; Catharine died in 1851, aged 37 years; Sara Maria became the wife of Upton Treat of Frankfort. Erasmus Archibald Jones was a man of fine education and abilities. He taught school and music and led the choir in the church on the hill from his earliest manhood. With the assistance of his father and Tisdale Dean and others he wrote a short history of his native town. He died in 1852 aged 31. Elmira, the widow of Ezra Treat, the only survivor of the family lives in Stillwater, Minnesota.

ALBERT LIVINGSTON KELLY

Albert Livingston Kelly, or as he was better known, to us, Esquire Kelly was born in the town of Bristol, New Hampshire, August 17, 1802, in the Fiske house.

In 1743 a coat of arms had been granted to the Honorable Robert Kelly of Doncaster, England. In southwestern England was a small parish of Kelly where a family of the name had lived for years on their manorial estate, even since the time of Henry II. Among the first of the name to come to New England was one, John Kelly, who settled in Newbury, Massachusetts in 1635.

The father of our townsman was Israel Webster Kelly of Goffstown, New Hampshire, who at the age of 19 held a commission under Alexander Hamilton in the Oxford War. Hamilton was on good terms with his officers, messed with them, and we are told that from this intercourse the young lieutenant became an "accomplished gentleman." In his later years he became a judge.

The mother of Albert Kelly was Rebecca Fletcher who was a daughter of the Reverend Elijah Fletcher. She was a woman of brilliant intellect. Her sister, Grace, became the wife of Daniel Webster. It was while she was visiting her sister, Mrs. Webster, in Salisbury that Mr. Kelly met her, and they were married at the Kelly home.

Often distinguished men met at this house, Eziekel Webster, Judge Richard Fletcher and others. Thus as a young man, Albert Kelly felt indirectly the personal charm of Hamilton, and later came in close contact with the master mind of Webster. And he was not less fortunate in his surroundings in later years.

He was sent to fitting school at Atkinson Academy, from which, at 15, he entered Dartmouth. From there he graduated in 1821; he had become proficient in Greek and held high rank, as a scholar.

He next went to Portland, Maine, where for three years he read law with the Honorable Stephen Longfellow and resided in his family, so that he knew the poet and his brothers. He always enjoyed referring to the life of those years, and to his acquaintance with this interesting family.

The year 1825 was important in his life; he was admitted to the Cumberland bar; he was chosen to deliver the fourth of July address at Portland, quite an honor for a man of 23; and he was appointed as agent in Frankfort to look after the claims of the Ten Proprietors' Grant.

It was thro Daniel Webster's influence that he received this appointment. It is said that when Mr. Webster recommended the young lawyer, he said, "I can't vouch for his experience but I can for his honesty and integrity."

As a lawyer here, he followed Philo Washburn, performed his duties as agent and became authority on all land and real estate laws — so that his counsel was widely sought. Then, too, he was interested in politics.

He married Caroline Peirce, a daughter of Waldo Peirce of the Marsh, in 1829. Nine children were born to them. It is an interesting fact that, as a young man, Mr. Kelly boarded at the Cox Tavern, kept by John Pike — the same house which is now the Kelly homestead; two sons, Frank and Silas, still occupy the old home. Its furniture, books and furnishings speak of early associations and of the taste of its owners. One son, Fitzroy Kelly, lives in Boston.

During Mr. Kelly's later years, Alexander Longfellow was often entertained by him. Daniel Webster, when on his Maine tour in 1835, was his guest for a few days; and to-day a portrait of the great statesman greets us in the front hall of the home.

THE NAME OF THOMPSON

A stranger to our village, on hearing this name, might at once think of the Benjamin Thompson of Massachusetts who figures in history as Count Rumford, who had become a tory in the Revolution; had gone within the British lines and was eventually sent to England by Lord Howe with important dispatches. However, his cleverness in later years, and his good to the world in general, overshadow this act and we forgive his turning to the enemy. We follow him to Bavaria where he became a powerful influence in military affairs. In Munich in 1790 he was knighted Count of the Holy Roman Empire and chose for his title the name of a New Hampshire town, Rumford, his early residence. He traveled on the continent, was interested in philosophical as well as political affairs, on which he wrote. He finally settled in Paris where his death occurred. He had been a member of the Royal Society of London and to it left prizes to be awarded for discoveries in light and heat. A chair at Harvard College known as the Rumford professorship was endowed by him: and in the city of Munich his statue adorns a public square.

It is not strange that we are interested in his life, for one of our first settlers was a cousin of his and bore the same name.

Our Benjamin Thompson — this branch of the family never bears a middle name — the son of Hiram Thompson, was born in Woburn, Massachusetts, November 15, 1774, in the Rumford house which is still standing in the north village.

As a young man he was a great reader, was fond of study and received some of his education with the future Count Rumford. He attended the old academy at Charlestown, and studied civil engineering. It was thro this subject that his attention was attracted to this distant plantation; he came here, assisted in laying out the town, traded in wood and bark, and finally settled. The house now owned by Ernest Damon was built by Mr. Thompson, and in 1800 he married Olive Oakman, a daughter of Tobias and Olive Oakman.

Mr. Oakman was a settler from Mansfield, Massachusetts who had put up a log hut on the site of the Tobias Thompson house. The old well under that house now is fed by the same spring which induced Mr. Oakman later to build a frame dwelling on the same spot.

Ten children were born to them at the little house in the lane. A younger daughter, Maria, was born in 1818. In 1840 she married Otis Kaler. Her son, James Otis Kaler is well known as a writer of boys' books under the name of James Otis. For a time he dwelt at the head of Kaler Street, but is now a resident of South Portland and is interested in schools as well as in letters. Some of the incidents of his stories took place in Frankfort and perhaps some of his characters are drawn from the lives of villagers.

Grandfather Thompson taught school here and "Marster Thompson" could wield other rods than the surveyor's.

Benjamin Thompson also served the town for many years as clerk, and when the British landed here in 1812 they paid his home a visit — not a pleasant one either, for they demanded the town papers of him. Upon refusing to give them up he was taken as prisoner to Castine.

There he was treated kindly so far as bodily comforts were concerned, but every means of speech was employed to force a surrender of the papers. He afterwards declared that he "could bear their insults far better than the thought that all the land between Castine and Bangor should fall into the hands of His Majesty." So he was detained there a prisoner of war for ten days, while his wife knew not whether he would be returned home or taken to the old country.

Of his sons, five were sea-faring men; two or three were masters of vessels and all but one of them were lost at sea.

There is a story still told of the son, William's first investment in vessel property. A Mr. Coburn and William Thompson bought an "old tub," the Jonas Hale. They took her to Treat's Mountain, loaded her with stone and when ready to sail had not decided upon who should be captain. So they drew straws and the office fell to Mr. Coburn. Then they got into an argument about which should remain aboard while the other went up town. But the newly chosen master settled it in short order. "I am captain and you are mate so you must stay," he said to young Thompson. After settling the balance of power, they finally set out for sea, but just off Drachm Point the craft sank and thus proved a profitless adventure.

Captain Thompson later commanded many large crafts; in the Compeer he went on voyages to Calcutta. Of this trip the log book says, "Jan 8, 1862 Thus we made the passage in 144 days from Boston Pilot to pilot in Calcutta, 33 souls in all on board." In the Amazon he went to Havana. His last voyage was in the Samuel Larrabee and the fate of the ship and her crew was never known.

A son of this Captain William Thompson was born in 1834 and was given the Rumford name, Benjamin Thompson.

He never sailed from this port, but this was his birthplace, and to it he came to spend the declining years of his life.

At an early age he began to go to sea; after his marriage to Miss Arabella Dunham, a daughter of George Dunham, the owner of uptown shipyards, his wife accompanied him on many long voyages, for he was a deep sea sailor.

The Progressive Age, a brig, was his first command, when he took her at Macao, China, to sail home.

An oil painting of one of the fast clippers, famous in the '50s, hangs in the dining-room at the Thompson home near Meeting House Hill. This is the Sportsman, "Captain Ben's" second vessel. Even in the picture she is going right along. The first voyage was to Buenos Ayres, the first year of the rebellion, and the return voyage proved very exciting. One morning just at daybreak, the mate reported a strange acting vessel in the distance. The captain went on deck. As the craft came nearer and nearer, it became evident that a privateer was on their track, — (war had been declared after they left that point, homeward bound). Realizing the possibility of capture, the captain sat right beside the wheelman to take advantage of wind and tide. Mrs. Thompson had secured the watches and valuables below and wanted the captain to go below, but he said: "No, my place is here." Winds, however, favored the Yankee vessel and she escaped. After their arrival in New York they learned of other crafts which had been chased and taken by the stranger.

This same Sportsman, was immediately chartered by our government and went to southern waters as a supply ship. The following letter, a testimonial to the young captain's service, is prized by Mrs. Thompson. It is framed and above it on the wall hangs the picture of its writer.

"Flagship Hartford
Western Gulf Blockading Squadron
Off Pensacola, Apr. 29. 1864

"Sir: Capt. Thompson commanded the ship Sportsman an ordnance store ship in my squadron, for upwards of two years and it gives me pleasure to say that he was always prompt in getting his vessel from place to place as required, kept her in good order, and was at all times ready to supply the wants of the squadron.

"Captain Thompson is a seaman & a gentleman and would no doubt make a good Volunteer officer in the Navy. Should it be his wish to enter the service as such, I would cheerfully recommend him to the favorable consideration of the Department.

Very respectfully
　　Your obedient servant
　　　　D. G. Farragut, Rear Admiral

"Hon Gideon Welles
　　Secretary of the Navy
　　　　Washington, D. C."

After the war Captain Thompson was master of other vessels and took many interesting voyages before his last Command, The Great Admiral. James Otis has made him the hero of The Boy Captains. Mrs. Thompson was a good sailor, too; she has been around the world three times; around the Cape of Good Hope six times; around Cape Horn fifteen times, once passing thro the Straits of LaMar. In her journal, she writes,

"Pacific Ocean Great Admiral 1876 Jan. 6 Ship going 10 knots; 58 days & just off Cape Horn, 11,000 miles from home. The days are long. Last night the sun set 15 minutes of 9 and rose at 3 this morning — twilight lasting all night."

On one voyage to Hong Kong, two ships were sailing along together. They ran into a typhoon, so tacked in different directions. One vessel was never heard from. But Captain Thompson was fortunate enough to reach port, with the sails of his ship blown into ribbons, altho he had bound them to the masts as he approached the storm. One poor sailor went crazy from fright in the experience. Mrs. Thompson also has a painting of this bark, as she entered the harbor from her perilous voyage.

Captain Thompson was considered "one of the safest and most experienced captains afloat," and in 1873 was put in command of the Great Admiral. This ship was built in East Boston for the Weld fleet. She was named for Farragut and carried a full length figure of the hero, under her bowsprit. The craft is now seen only in Pacific waters, and since in a few years no vessels of her kind will be seen, a picture of her is interesting.

"The Admiral is 1576 ton burden, 214 feet length of keel, 226 feet over all, 40 feet 6 inch beam and 20 feet 6 inch depth of hold. Her after cabin is finished in mahogany, rosewood and satinwood paneling, picked in with gilt and is upholstered in wine-colored plush. On the port side of the cabin is a medicine store and adjoining this is the linen locker. On the larboard side are staterooms, book locker, and bath-room, the latter fitted up with all necessary conveniences and finished in black walnut. Aft the cabin are the captain's private apartments. Forward on the larboard side stand the staterooms, and the officers' quarters opening from the dining room. The galley is one of the most convenient and roomy ever placed upon a sailing ship and her carpenter shop contains all the appliances and tools necessary for such work as may be needed on the voyage. Fresh water is obtained by means of a condenser capable of supplying fifty gallons per hour. The engine used for the purpose also gives motive power for hoisting the sails and raising anchors. In short, the entire equipment of the vessel, combined with her great strength, render her in the opinion of navigators, one of the safest crafts afloat."

From the Philadelphia "North American."

She made several quick passages, one from Hong Kong to Liverpool in 34 days.

Captain Thompson's last days were spent in retirement at Winterport, except for occasional visits to Boston. There he was always welcomed by his old friends as "The Commodore." He had been a good sailor, good to his sailors, a good business man and a smart captain. He was always an interesting and entertaining companion, and the passing of this gentleman of the old school was with deep regret to his many friends.

X - Old Furniture— Tea Tables and Their Appointments

Many collectors of antiques would consider themselves fortunate if they could get some of the interesting pieces of furniture which have outlived their original owners or surroundings in Winterport, stored in some attic, shed or barn; or surviving in some long closed house. A good old table may be in use, in kitchen or milkroom and seem to be of little value; but, if the owner is asked to part with it for money, the true value is very quickly revealed. Some bit of history or sentiment attached to this or that article makes it priceless and the collector departs empty handed. Thus the housewife saves money in her own way and is satisfied.

There are bureaus and chests of drawers of endless variety. The most common bureau is the one known as "heavy style" which has two twisted posts, each surmounted by a carved pineapple, on either side of the drawers. The front finish is a veneer. A few slant top bureau desks are still in use, some as they were first made, and some restored, with brass finishings.

Many four-poster beds have been consigned to wood piles or have served as kindling; but now and then one is found in an attic, "saved to be done over and used sometime." Relics of one bridal dowry, sent from Massachusetts, an Eastlake bureau and a canopy top four-poster of pineapple design with an additional elaborate carving of weeping willow, are still kept.

In one home, a field bed is in use — dressed in keeping with its age. These beds have a top which suggests the shape of a tent, hence the name. Cords take the place of modem springs and help to hold its mahogany frame together. Home made sheets cover the feather ticks; hand woven blankets are over these. A pink "comforter" backed with quilted linen gives additional warmth; and over all is a blue and red chintz coverlid, with squares cut from the comers to make it fit around the large posts. The coverlid is made from the original hangings of the bed.

There are many different kinds of candle tables; one, a small square top was supported on four slender legs; another, with the same kind of top was held on a single rod which crowned four curved legs; and still another, with four curved legs, had an arrangement so that its top might be turned up, thus becoming an ornament. The passing of the candle has given these over to various purposes now; one may hold a glass of tissue paper flowers, or be covered with flower pots; another may be gilded or given a coat of white paint. Whether they came from over the water or from the hand of a local cabinet maker, yet few remain as they were first made.

A "Four Poster" (Still in use)

Square sewing tables, whose leaves hug two small drawers, have neat little compartments to accommodate needles, thread and sewing material.

The card tables are of peculiar make; round when extended and semicircular when folded; when not in use for their destined purpose they graced the best room, placed so that one leaf rested against the wall, while on the other leaf, supported by the legs, were knicknacks; a glass lamp surmounting a brass rod which was fastened into a base — a succession of onyx blocks; a card receiver of pieces of cardboard, silk bound, which were worked in cross stitch; and a small case of wax flowers.

Larger tables seem not to have shared the humiliating fate of their kindred, the candle-stand; but have been promoted to places of honor. Now, too good for a dining-room, for which they were intended, they occupy living-room, sitting-room, parlor, or even the front entry. They are of every shape and pattern; square, oblong or round; their corners, square or rounded; the feet, claw or club; legs, spindle or cabriole; all the styles of which you read are found here.

One former kitchen table occupies the comer of a front hall. In its early days it lived in Plymouth in the home of a Calvin preacher. No doubt many knotty questions were discussed over its leaves, by noted divines of that day; and the descendants of John Alden, with colonial officials dined from it.

Another, so proud of its shining top that only a card receiver rests on its polished surface, greets you on entering a front door. This is "Grandmother Avery's." When the British took possession of Castine, the officers made themselves at home and used the Avery family silver and china. Each daughter of this family became the possessor of what she called a British cup and saucer. The cups are odd looking ones — coffee cups large like a bowl, of dark blue ware, covered with a shell and deep sea tangle pattern, and around the top a narrow yellow band.

But the family china, which survived the war and the English occupation, according to the early custom, has passed to the oldest daughter's descendants; and is now owned by Mrs. Harriet Abbott, granddaughter of Captain Thatcher and Hannah Atkins Avery of North Castine, who ordered it from Liverpool before 1812 thro a Captain Higgins.

There is a sugar bowl, tea or water pot and creamer; but there are no plates as pewter ones were used.

The ware is white and very thin; the small bowl shaped cups are without handles; the saucers are very deep. They have a bold decoration; a large red rose set in green foliage, across whose leaves is a dash of red. A black line edged with a purple beading forms a border. Above the pattern is the large monogram — in black — T H A (Thatcher and Hannah Avery.)

A good housewife always cared for her own china, washing it with her own hands, in a wooden tub or keeler, used only for the china. So this set is still complete. When any of the younger generation visit at Abbott place, they are always served to a cup of tea from this choice ware.

As the friends of Mrs. Abbott have called on her in later years, they have been quite sure to find her in the brown south room, comfortably seated in a big willow chair, book in hand, in front of Grandmother Avery's picture. This is a painting copied from a portrait on glass, done by Mr. Greenleaf about 1815 or 1820.

As a child I was always awed by the picture and wondered if the person were man or woman, and I always expected the strong face to turn and look at me, so pleasant seemed the eyes. The dark dress, covered at the neck by a white kerchief seemed like man's attire. The dark hair just showing beneath a little net cap, dotted with clovers, proclaims the young matron; for, after the English fashion, as soon as our maids became wives they donned the cap in token of their honor. Pleasant indeed it must have been to share her hospitality and ready wit of which her daughters inherited such a goodly share.

One table which is now a parlor center table, came from an Oak Point home. It bears on its top a depression made by a bullet which was sent from a British musket thro the window, and glanced across the table, but left the family unharmed.

"Shouldn't wonder a mite if 'twas a hundred.

"It's been in the house ever since I can remember.

"Folks you know couldn't keep house in them days without a set of chiny.

"Think sometime when I'm smart I'll get some old ladies to take tea with me and use the old chiny."

Thus explained an old lady of seventy-seven as she shook her white curls and bustled about, opened the sitting-room closet door and took from the top shelf "mother's tea set." Of its pieces, — a dozen cups and saucers, a sugar bowl, creamer, water pot, bowl and two cake plates — but one has ever been broken. That is the handle of the sugar bowl, and that is saved.

The ware is pure white decorated in lilac colored design, a bunch of peach-peaches and their foliage alternating with a bunch of roses.

For the best china the best table was used tho really a card table of mahogany. The edge is inlaid with a strip of bird's eye maple marked on either side with a fine ebony thread. Now it is over a hundred years old, is not marred and has never been re-polished.

"I can remember when I was a little bit of a girl," she added. "My mother set it for company for tea and set it with the old chiny. O no! I didn't sit down, there wasn't room for us children. Children had to wait in them days."

There is in the town one dining-room of real old style, every detail preserved without the introduction of modern ideas. Enter it from the front

Mothers Tea Set and the Best Table

room and the first thing you will notice is the two foot high mantel over its huge black fireplace. The room is painted an old, old soft gray, the yard-high hand-finished wainscoting and the woodwork of its many doors; for from it you may go to porch, kitchen, bedroom, front room, closet, front hall, attic and storeroom.

The long table still stands in front of the fireplace spread to its greatest extent just as it stood when the owner entertained there the selectmen of the town; or when the big family were all at home and each of the five girls had her own work to do and it was no "put out" to have seventeen walk in to dinner unannounced.

As you depart thro the covered porch you are offered a drink from the well over which the house is built, and then passing thro the vine covered door you pass from an old world into the new.

XI - House Furnishings and Firesides

The earliest houses were naturally of the style most easily built and of materials most easily obtained; therefore, the first home of a white settler, here as elsewhere in the colonies was the log hut, for which tree trunks were stripped and piled up to form a shelter. These did for home until the surrounding land could be cleared a little, and then a more substantial dwelling was erected. Some went up the river to Wheeler's Mills for lumber; some down to Marsh Mills, rafting the materials to this place; while some cut and finished the lumber on their own claims.

These first frame dwellings were the low story and a half cottage; patterned after the old Plymouth style — many of which may be seen to-day in Massachusetts or Connecticut towns. These, with low gently sloping roof, resembled bird houses, set with the longest side toward the river.

Many of the first houses have reached the hundred year mark and have survived the ravages of time — because they were built of strong material and finished as needed, slowly: the building of the old Goodwin home, already referred to, shows how slowly.

Often the living-room and bedroom were the only ones finished for years — the chambers left unfinished or "open" until the increase in size of family and wherewithal saved by hard labor, demanded, and allowed the luxury of lath and plaster.

The location of the old houses shows the path of settlement from one end of the plantation to the other; from the home of Moses Baker above Cove Hill to the Blaisdell house at the southern end.

At the top of Sabine Hill and a little to the east of the present main road, set the log cabin of Paul Downs. He was a lumberman, owned some oxen and by wood hauling, and plowing for his neighbors, was soon able to supplant this cabin by a frame house which stood just in front of the little black weatherbeaten cottage now occupied by his grandson, Benjamin Nichols.

From there the main thoroughfare ran to Oak Point, passed the Stubbs homestead, which was taken down, only a few years ago; and along to the high point where stood the Daten house, which was associated with the Kempton name. This commanded an unobstructed view up and down the river.

On a side hill set Nehemiah Rich's house. From its windows the inmates could look out across Kempton's Cove and daily at low tide they could see the wreck of the flagship Warren as she washed to pieces on the flats. This house in after years was moved on to the main road, north of the Hacket woods. It was then owned by William Page and is still standing, tho completely hidden by lilac bushes and woodbine.

Simeon Kenney when he stopped teaching school in the village, to become a farmer, chose the next eminence to the south of the Richs' as his home. This building is still in good condition and is known as the "Ford house."

The "Old Goodwin house," "Lombard house" and "Norton house" stood not far apart to the south: the two latter are still standing.

The road continued past the Tommy Johnston house in a direct line across the Thompson land. A grandchild of Mr. Thompson remembers the old farmhouse before any improvements were made on it: when it had a big fireplace, the great crane with pots and kettles hanging on it.

The Blaisdell house, the oldest in town, is kept in nearly every particular as it used to be.

Tho many of these structures were unpainted, yet Nature did her work well and to-day some wear the silver gray coats which are only made by time and weather. A few were coated with whitewash and one or two perhaps boasted of paint but for ornamentation they depended mostly upon the plots of gay flowers by the door — perhaps peonies from a Plymouth garden, or a brier rose from the cape.

Many public houses were scattered thro the country, built on the same plan as dwelling houses but much larger.

The homes which the settlers provided for their animals were much more pretentious than their own shelter. The barns were often twice the size of the houses and the "barn raising" was as important a social event as that of the house: neighbors from all about the country attended: often the frame was set up at noon, thus allowing the morning for the gathering of friends and the afternoon for festivities and visiting.

A shed attached to the house sometimes formed a passageway to the big barn back of it. Here was the home of the winter's wood, the storehouse for farm tools, and the indispensable iron kettle: and on the rafters were hung the shad and smelt nets, after the season's work was done.

If we are invited to enter these houses by the front door, we find ourselves in an entry — small and square — a veritable box. From it open doors into the north and south rooms, the fourth side often leading to a closet. The back stairs answered all the purposes of the family and generally led from the pantry or milk-room to the upper floor — to open chambers and the boys' bedrooms.

One house, built in 1791, had no lathed bedroom for eight years. The room was then plastered immediately, three days being needed for the job. Surely improvements were appreciated in those days. The south room was finished first, and used as a "keeping room" or "living room," unless the kitchen in the rear of the house was used for family gatherings.

There was a generous supply of closets: always a large clothes press: a china closet, which in thrifty families was supplied with glass doors: all sorts and sizes of closets about the mantel and fireplace: mysterious and surprise closets within closets, for medicine, for linen, for eatables and we know not what else. Access to these was gained by turning a little brass button, which revolved on a brass plate set in the woodwork of the door frame. A brass knob on the door served for ornament.

The larger doors were fitted with various kinds of handles and latches, brass, iron, pewter, or wooden: the hinges were often hand cut and of styles best liked by the owners. In one house alone, I saw seven different patterns of latches, and one latchstring.

The interior woodwork was more elaborate than you would expect, knowing that it was all done by hand. Ornaments used were finely grooved lines, square blocks with carved edges, tiny blocks used as beading, and some scroll work. When larger houses were built large hallways were introduced and with them the need of elaborate decoration of doorways, stairways and wainscoting.

The Dunton house or old Chick house was originally a hip-roofed house and still has the large front hall. On either side of the front door are side lights — and over it is a fan-shaped window which lights up the ten foot wide hall, which once ran directly thro the house. The combined height of upper and lower hall is about twenty feet. At the left, a short flight of steps leads to a landing — and turning, you go to the upper hall by a second flight. A copy of the original paper covers the wall, — gray brown mottled paper, in imitation of large oblong granite blocks.

But the woodwork merits close attention. Along the sides of the hall and up the wall beside the steps is a wainscoting, a couple of feet high. Along its base is a narrow baseboard. Its top is finished with a molding formed of long horizontal strips of wood between which are set at intervals, three vertical

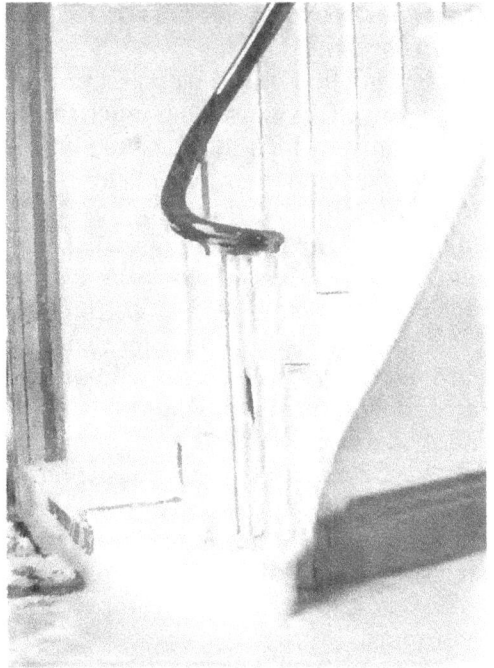

A Wattling Stairway

blocks (three inches wide). These are painted red and form a beading. The same finish is used near the ceiling in place of a paper border. At the outer edge of the stairs is a molding and the end of each step is fitted with a double scroll of wood. The newel post and banister are of plain dark wood.

Perhaps the most artistic stairway in town is the one whose graceful curves speak for themselves in the picture. It is a winding stairway, a baluster for each step and each step extending out a little over the lower one.

At the Tobias Thompson house the straight stairway is guarded by a severely plain balustrade and newel posts. These are made from ironwood which "Captain Tobias" brought from Russia.

When the luxury of plaster became more common, the next need was a wall covering or decoration: and as many captains went abroad many of the first wallpapers came from foreign countries. Of course only the well-to-do people could have them. Three hallways in town for years were covered with paper like the picture; the bridge and the tower were brown; the water, green. A roll of this paper, paste and all, as it was removed from the wall of the Thompson house to give place to a newer style, is stowed in the attic. In the north room of the same house was a paper of large figure — a man crossing a bridge. During an illness, Captain Thompson occupied that room and he ordered the paper removed, "For," he said, "I can't rest till that paper is removed; it makes me so tired to see that man keep goin' across that bridge."

Fifty years ago, the Lathly Rich house had one room papered with this leaf paper. The leaves are a foot and a half long, are cream edged with gold against a green velvety background. It was bought in Glasgow for Mr. Rich by an Orrington captain who was in his employ.

In one house is the "Governor's room" so called because governors and men of note have occupied it: the governors. Marble, Robie and Bodwell: Hannibal Hamlin, when vice-president: J. G. Blaine when a member of Congress: and later Seth Milliken and Eugene Hale. The paper on the walls of this room has been described by the owner thus: "some one stood in the middle of the floor and threw whitewash at the wall," — so striking are the big white leaves against the bright blue background.

One house has marvelous door decorations. The woodwork is painted with white enamel, and hand-decorated with gold. Each upper panel in the doors and the original window shutters, is the background for a scene painted in oil in an oval surrounded by scroll work. There are nearly thirty of these scenes, each picturing sky, hills, water, one tree and a castle, arranged differently. The mistress of the house is wont to say: "all is not gold that glitters," for the mere sight of this gilt causes consternation in the heart of every maid she can employ and she finds herself alone with the pictures, gold lines and her housework.

Most of the hip-roofed houses have been changed to the pointed roof: the Little Tavern and the Fred Atwood homestead. Some follow the original plan, the Dudley house, Washburn, Kelly and Belches homes. When the last one was built there was no house between it and the river: its present owner, who was born in the house and has passed her eighty years there, can remember when no building stood on either side of the road between it and the Jones residence, except the old Sampson house and barn. The Belches house sets in the old garden at the foot of Whig street near Main and remains as it was built eighty-three years ago, except for the loss of its big chimney.

The daily tasks performed in these homes were about the same as those of all New England households. Each season brought its own work and domestic cares.

Thompson House

Governor's Room

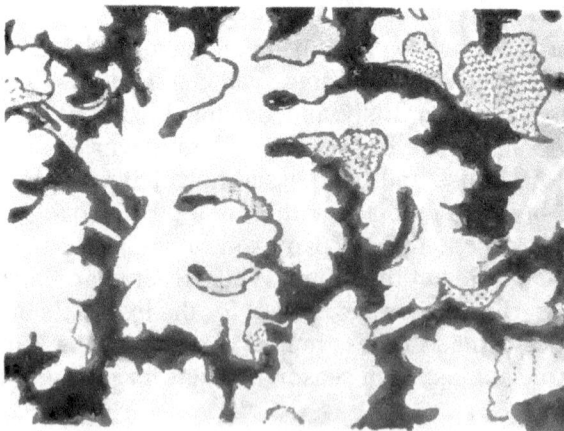

Rich Cottage, Dean Street

Old Wall Papers

With the coming of spring the need of a tonic was felt and in the preparation of it the younger members of the family could help. Chick Common was the base of supplies and there the children were sent for juniper boughs, yellow root, sassafras root, box berry or "ivory" leaves and spruce boughs. Nearer home was dug dandelion root, and mother had the wash boiler ready to receive them all. They were half covered with water, boiled and strained: then molasses and yeast added to the liquor, and, after "working" for a few days it was transformed into a beverage that "tasted so good" — old-fashioned spruce beer.

Before house cleaning time the soft soap must be made. The winter's hard wood ashes, which had been accumulating, were now put into the leach tub which would hold a number of barrels. Hot water was poured over them till it soaked thro, then cold water, while pails were set under it to catch the drippings or lye. Sometimes it was a slow process and must stand all night before it began to run. Meanwhile the large iron kettle, into which had been put scraps of soap grease and potash was set out doors over the fire. The lye was turned into this and the whole mixture "biled," till it roped, when it was "done." This was the year's supply of soap and was used for everything except the bath.

Even if the mothers did always have to work, at times there would be a surprise for the big family of boys, which had been away to work. For several days before their return mother would do extra cooking. She had planned to dress up and invite them to tea — to bring out the best linen and dishes — to show them that she could entertain if she had the time and opportunity. It was the little things like this which made her boys big and manly — these were the things remembered when at her death bed, strong men could pledge themselves that for her memory, none bearing their name should ever come to want.

Mary Andrews — Her Sampler

There was quilting, plaiting of straw and bleaching bonnets, spinning and weaving, knitting and candle making for long summer days and winter evenings.

Sometimes the quilting frames were set up out of doors, and around them the ladies gathered for a "bee" at which tongues worked as nimbly as fingers.

Bleaching bonnets always suggests the name of Aunt Hannah Ferrin. She was a devout little maiden lady who lived in a cottage on Church street and who earned a living by sewing straw or plaiting grasses into bonnets. Then she hung them in a barrel to be bleached with smoking sulphur which had been set in the bottom of it. The barrel was covered but they had to be looked at every now and then to see that they didn't burn. To children she was "the old woman who swept the cobwebs from the sky" and they loved dearly to go and see her.

There is a story told of the time of the Dunstable straw bonnets. A maiden lady, Betsey Lane, was "help" for thirteen years in the family of Mr. Elisha Chick. "Help" then meant one of the family. At one time her employer had for sale at his store a box of these bonnets. Now Betty was a strict Methodist and thought it wrong to wear bows or flowers — but these bonnets she liked and wanted one very much. But the price, $7, was beyond her means. Her employer, in fun, told her that if on next Sabbath she would wear one to Universalist meeting he would give it to her. To his surprise and the surprise of every one else, on Sunday morning, Betty walked into church, arrayed in the big bonnet — bows and furbelows were missing for she wore just a ribbon under her chin for strings.

The story of the spinning wheel has been told over and over again — how our grandmothers carded the wool and spun the yam for dresses as well as for the family stockings and blankets: how the farmers raised their own flax and the wives spun the thread and wove their own linen.

Each improvement in the art of candle-making came to us — from the primitive way — a long stick suspended over a tub, along which were twisted pieces of wicking — to various kinds of molds — which produced more and made work lighter. The winter evenings spent in helping mother, when childish hands could hold the ball of wicking, fasten it in the tubes or gather drippings from the tub of cold water — these are all a pleasant memory now, tho not fully appreciated then.

Hand Embroidered Clothes

The hands that could do all of these useful tasks could also turn to careful and dainty needlework, for the making of patchwork and samplers was taught to children of six or eight years.

We wonder if it were fun for little Caroline Rich, aged eight in 1817, to work the stitches which, a hundred years later, we so much admire — even when the cross stitches were in pretty colored silks and when mother had woven the golden linen for her to work on. The careful hemstitching, the embroidery trees and plants must have sometimes been put in with a sigh because she wanted to go out to play.

Or this sampler of Mary Andrews: did she sometimes shed a tear over the long black lines which must be worked in before she could put in the gay colored letters; or did she work with joy because she was sure to play when the day's stent was done? Dear little girls, now remembered best as "grandmother Rich" or "Aunt Caroline!"

One woman tells that she knit a pair of stockings before she was five years old. "O," she said, "mother always brought her children up to knit a pair of stockings before they were four or five, as her mother had been brought up, and her grandmother before her. Mother always made it a rule never to speak of anyone unless she could say something good."

Children were brought up in those days.

So the young women could do all kinds of embroidery on fine linen, for underwear — nightgowns and night caps of every description. And when the wedding day came, no dressmaker had fashioned the gown, bands and kerchiefs, but her own deft fingers had made the cloth, made the gown and all the trimmings. And when children came to the new home, the mother's own hand had made the little garments and caps — decorating them in eyelet work, with little leaves or clovers.

Now and then it happened that the wedding gown and its accessories came from abroad. Can you imagine Jane Prince Robbins attired in a dress of this gay pattern? This breadth is perhaps a yard long — a white ground. The thick foliage of the trees is half covered with two big chrysanthemum-like blossoms. At its foot are green leaves and foliage on a brown ground, crossed by a green fence. The same pattern is repeated in different colors, in blue-green or yellow-green. There is a

Wedding Gown of Jane Prince Robbins

story that this gown just missed being a wedding dress a second time. Years after the death of Mr. Goodwin's wife, he presented it to a friend of the family, for a wedding dress. The prospective bride was at the washtub one morning when her future husband came along. When he saw her washing, with the sleeves rolled back from the pretty white arms, he wanted her to go immediately to be married. So she went from her washing to her wedding and the dress was not used on that occasion — but in after years it appeared now and then at a ball.

In these home pictures, we must not forget the dogs: for in that day they were as much a part of the family as the children were. Carlo Andrews, Trusty Jones, Tiger Rich and Cassius Washburn were important members of those households. After Mr. Washburn's death, Cassius forsook the house and attached himself to a Mr. Page, following closely at his heels. His mistress would sometimes catch him and carry him into the house to cook meat for him — but this attention did not make up for the loss of a master and he would run to the gutter for food.

The streets of the old town were quiet — that quiet which makes itself felt on warm mornings in summer in our New England towns. Everyone had gone to church, when a rap came at the door. There stood a stout old lady who nodded me a cheerful "good day, miss." I knew her not for she was out of the past and her face was concealed in a big green calash, two feet in circumference, which, as she nodded her head in conversation, nodded too in each of the separate rows of shirring and in each separate ruffle. The bridle held it in place, and at the same time she gathered the ends of her shawl on her bosom. This soft brown crepe shawl was edged with heavy embroidery and its folds and deep fringe fell nearly to the bottom of the poplin gown, of black and brown check, which completed the costume.

It all belonged to grandmother and the green barege calash was her "meetin bunnit" made by her, only to be worn as best. Quite fitting it seemed on this Sabbath for her granddaughter to step back into a picture of a hundred years ago.

XII - In '55

In the middle of the last century Frankfort was a flourishing business town. A newspaper of that time describes it as having "abundant wharves, numerous shipyards already renowned to the ends of the earth for the magnificent structures they have given to the seas, lumber manufactories, driven by steam which cease not their din day nor night for the greater part of the year."

In 1855 its waterfront was fringed by twelve wharves. The ruins of them show quite a difference in construction from those of to-day. A box was made by driving piles into the mud, the center was filled in with cross logs and covered with rocks and gravel. Their flaw in construction is plainly shown in the way they have gone to pieces — the logs supporting the sides have fallen over, decayed or washed away, thus leaving no support for the heavy rocks.

There were two piers at the steam mill; one at the foot of Marine street; two wharves of the Union Company at Whig street; Dean's at Ferry street; two owned by Lathly Rich at Willow and Commercial streets; Williams' just south of Washington street; and J. Riche's just north of it; and Reeds wharf.

One of the finest views in our town is from the old Holmes house. From this point, toward the south, are long fields, the still densely wooded Treat Point, and in the distance the dark top of Mt. Waldo and the sister mountains Heagan and Musketon. In clear weather Fort Knox may be discerned just at the farther end of the big bay which spreads out at the foot of the elm-bordered street

On a Clear Day; Fort Knox in the Distance

leading down to the shore. Here, what a difference between the scene of today and that of half a century ago. We, whose memory cannot go back to that time can scarcely realize the changes the years have wrought in the picture. Now, a stretch of water, a veritable inland lake, an old weir on yonder point, and the worn piles of a tumble-down wharf at the river brink are but capital for the artist. This is all that remains to mark the site of the old steam mill, which was once a busy center for manufacturing lumber.

Mr. Theophilus Cushing was head of the firm which carried on this large business, the various departments of which employed about a hundred men. Cushing and Company's wharves consisted of two piers; a large one just south of Holmes street and a smaller one below. A long boom or pound for logs extended along the shore above the main wharf and was protected by a small breakwater. This breakwater was opposite the Morrissy house. On the main wharf was a saw mill, and near by was the company's blacksmith shop.

The shore road, or Oak street, then extended farther south, and at its junction with Holmes street was the store and office building. The company's boarding-house was near by. Mr. Cushing began this plant in 1841; it was the largest establishment of its kind in town, and manufactured long lumber, sugar box shooks, laths, clapboards, soap and candle boxes. An extensive business was carried on for years. Then it was discontinued, and several years later the buildings were destroyed by fire. The steam mill property included Hardy's Point, which was sometimes called steam mill farm. Part of the British fleet anchored in this locality in 1812, on one of their searching parties. The British sloop Sylph grounded and was hauled off here. To lighten her, a number of cannon balls were thrown overboard. Two prominent men of the town happened to be near enough to be able to locate them. The next night after the departure of the sloop, at low water, one of the men was on hand in a gondola and secured them. The second man claimed part of them as his share, but without success.

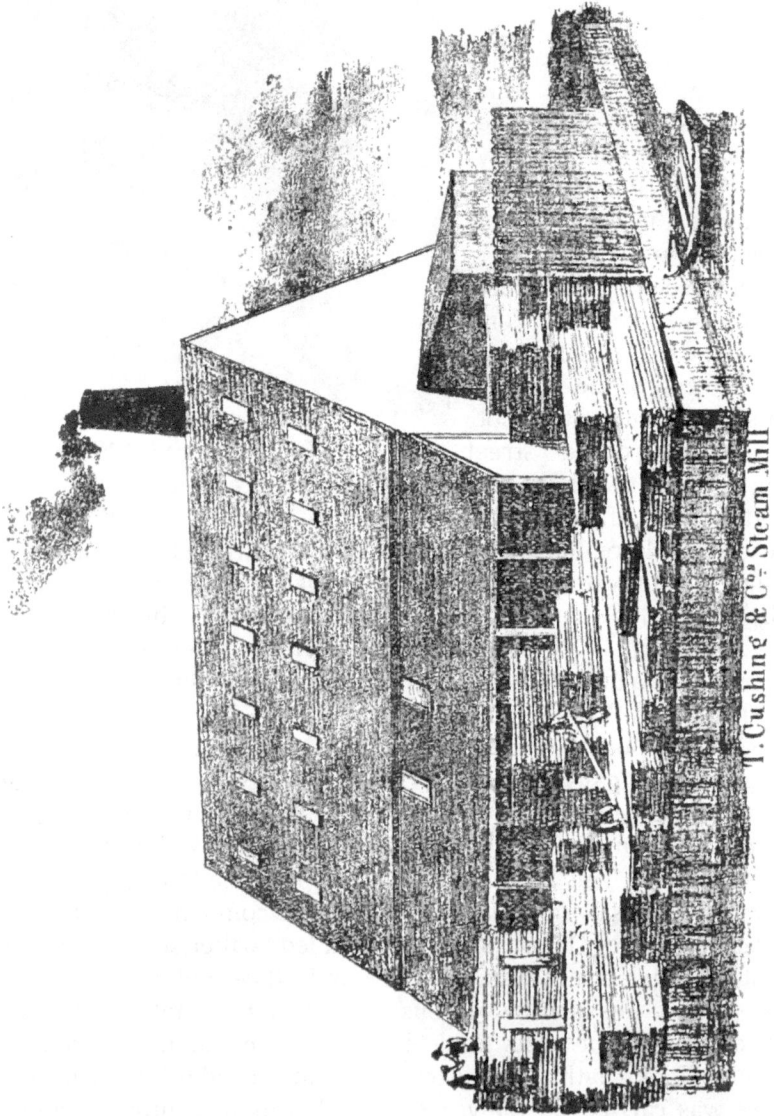

T. Cushing & Co's Steam Mill

It was thought wise to keep a night watch while the Sylph lay here. Mr. Archibald Jones was one of those to take a turn. Those who were with him proposed to range along the shore and see what had come on shore from her. They found a barrel of rosin, a cake of tallow, a piece of rope, and a water pail.

There were originally two wharves at the foot of Mechanic street. One was Lindsey's wharf and the firm of Folsom and Lindsey did business here.

A chain factory was at the Lindsey wharf, owned by the company of Sproul, Cushing and Kelley. After the business ran out the building was used as a foundry for the manufacture of the old-fashioned Hampden stoves.

This also may have been the wharf known as "Mollie Hall Wharf" for at one time, Mrs. Hall who occupied a cottage near George Grant's house, moved into the upper rooms of Lindsey's storehouse. She was a well-known town character — her name appearing in the local phrase — "to have no more 'scretion than Mollie Hall's pig."

Mrs. Hall afterward married a Bowden, and became the mother of Robert, or "Bob Bodden," as he was called, who endeared himself to all the young people of the neighborhood by his unending fund of stories, especially his yarns about the famous "Good Ship Rover."

It was near this wharf that the old mourning ring was found.

The second wharf close by was sometimes known as the Little wharf. Two vessels were built here. The brig Caroline Kelley was one of them. The bark Wild Pigeon was also built here. Mr. Jones says that James Little had a brig loaded with lumber at his wharf, which was taken to Liverpool as a prize by the British (1814).

The Union Company, which was composed of business men of the town, found that they needed a large wharf, so constructed the present steamboat wharf. It was the landing-place for Portland steamers and Edward Fernald was agent. In 1864 there were four buildings on Union wharf, one cooper shop, one blacksmith shop and two storehouses. The company finally sold out to Amos Sproul, hence it is sometimes called Sproul's wharf. Then Treat and Company bought it, and it again became a business center. They had a big shipyard on the north side of the wharf and several crafts were launched here, the brig Robin among others. The company put up the large building on Main street now occupied by J. F. Hussey. They were large importers of sugar and molasses from the West Indies, and of hides and wool from South America. Besides the coopering business they carried on an extensive shipping trade. Possibly old sailors could tell interesting yams of hairbreadth escapes with lives and booty in the days of smuggling.

In 1860 Messrs. Lord and Eveleth purchased the foundation of the Dean wharf, made improvements, enlarged it, built a large storehouse and installed a hay press there. They pressed hay for the government in war time. Portland steamers, the City of Richmond, T. F. Secor, and the Lady Lang stopped here. The name of the latter was painted on the storehouse, and this landing was then called the Lady Lang wharf.

It was here, long afterward, that the eleven, twelve and fourteen ton pieces of the soldier's monument were landed, and here came the twenty yokes of oxen and many horses to take it to Oak Hill Cemetery.

The most interesting incident to occur here of late years, was during the high tide of ___, when the water was high over the spiling and flooded the river road and nearby buildings. One man rowed a boat up into Captain Clifford's shed. The receding tide left ice cakes weighing tons in the road. At this time, the Vandalia (locally called "the old Vandeelia"), was landed on to the southern side of the wharf. And for once she followed the career of the warship whose name she bears and "rode the high seas."

The present Ferry wharf was built by Benjamin Shaw, and later passed in turn into the hands of Lathly Rich, George Crockett and Charles Rich, whose heirs sold it to the Winterport Ferry Company.

The McKenney wharf was at one time owned by Lathly Rich, and was a great shipping center. It was an especially busy place during the fall. Being the terminus, the "winter port" for boats, all freight landed here and was teamed to Bangor, and passenger service was by coach. The steamship company was then called the Sanford Independent Line. It was afterward known as the Boston and Bangor Steamship Company, and is now the Eastern Steamship Company.

A letter of April 1847, says: "It has been constant sledding till the 10th of the month, the river is not open yet, & we have had 4 boats in at a time from Boston." And again, "The boats are crowding into Frankfort, Coaches & Stages are crammed and crowded full."

At the foot of Dean street were two yards run by George and Isaac Dunham. One yard was above and the other below the wharf; and a long list of vessels can be given which were turned off these stocks. The Volunteer, a newspaper of '63 mentions that, "L. Rich, Esq., is getting out in Canada the frame of a fore and aft schooner of about 400 tons burthen, and will soon commence its building in the Dunham yard."

Mr. Rich had a number of vessels constructed here. They were named for himself and for members of his family, — May A., Mary B., Annie A., Carrie M. and Lath Rich — the Rich fleet. He finally bought the property of the Dunhams. The lower yard extended up across the road and a vessel was built and launched in the hollow south of George Crockett's house.

The storehouse was used in war time as barracks for the soldiers. The first company from Frankfort stayed here till they were called into service.

Above Dunham's yard was the Arey and Williams wharf. This firm also built many vessels. I have been told that between these two yards three ships at a time might be seen on the stocks.

It was at this yard that the Bone and Muscle Society began its work. This was a company of ten or twelve men — carpenters and others — who were to work together, do all labor, and share the profits. They started to build one vessel, but too much money was needed for their project, so she was put up at auction. Treat and Company purchased and finished her and named her the Alpine.

At the J. Rich wharf shipbuilding was done.

Upon our shore, opposite the little church at North Bucksport, there has been until within a few years a large granite house. It was grewsome with its gaping windows, was said to be haunted, and no children playing on this shore ever dared to enter it. Below was the old stone wharf or the Reed wharf and the adjoining land is known as the "Reed Place." Originally this was owned by a company which at first did a thriving business. Above the main road on the eminence is a granite quarry which was worked then. There was a blacksmith shop which employed six or seven men. From the quarry to the wharf was a railroad and the landing was equipped with derricks and conveniences for handling stone.

Captain William Reed of Bucksport bought out the company and added a cooper shop. Then he went into shipbuilding, and in '53 built the Isabella Jewett. Her model was in the Reed store on the Main road until within a few years.

During a September gale, a schooner, the Eastern Bell, was dragged from the village and tipped over at this wharf. This may have given rise to the story current that the first vessel Captain Reed built came into the river loaded with coal, and sunk at the wharf on the day of his death.

Of the twelve wharves mentioned, only four are now in use — the steamboat, Eveleth's, the Ferry and McKenney's.

Considering this decrease in the importance of the town, a newcomer naturally asks the cause of the change. There is no answer ready, but the feeling of the older citizens may be expressed in the words of an old river workman — "I feel lonesome on the river now."

XIII - Smelt Fishing

This locality may add to the Century Dictionary. A search there for the word smelter showed that it is used only in connection with the iron industry. But we have smelters of a very different kind — the men who give us one of the choicest of table delicacies, the smelt. It is said that these tiny fish are so named because of their peculiar odor, like violets. We, who eat these dainties, do not realize the labor and danger with which the fishermen are beset. There are acts of daring and heroism, done here on our river by men who follow the occupation and, in mid-winter, set their nets for a livelihood, which are never recorded.

The smelt fisher has a vocabulary, all his own, which is most interesting if he chooses to explain it.

The first smelting near us was done at Hampden, and the oldest fisherman there was Joe Higgins — "uncle Joe," his mates called him.

At the Cove, ice fishing was carried on. When the river froze over, the fisherman went to mid-river on the ice, cut holes in it and set his nets. The square mesh net was used, one about thirty feet by ten, such as seiners took in drifting for shad or alewives. They were hand knit over a mesh board, of about one and one-eighth inch mesh, as size of fish demanded. The nets were fastened by their four comers to two long poles, which were then let perpendicularly through the opening in the ice till they nearly touched the river bed. All along the New England coast smelts were caught in this way. On the Piscataqua, boys used to put up a tent (forerunner of our fish camp), over a five or eight foot hole, warm themselves by an oil lamp and comfortably await a catch.

Open water fishing was begun off our shore and in this "Cap'n" Joe Arey was the pioneer. Joe Stubbs was his partner but later sold out to Loren Jepson; every fisherman has a partner, for two strong men are needed to handle the gear.

A more elaborate equipment was needed for this kind of fishing: an anchor, frame, scow, net and the fish camp.

A camp, just large enough to contain a bunk, a stove and a chair or two, was set on the shore near the owner's fishing privilege. Sometimes it was shingled and sometimes just laid over with boards, and near it was generally a pile of hardwood or of driftwood. This was the temporary home of the fisherman during the smelting season. A few camps or shacks are now at the steam mill wharf, and near the steamboat wharf. Many have been removed from the latter place, but years ago there were three times as many as now. A man who looked at a recent photograph of this miniature village, said: "Uncle Joe's camp ain't there any longer."

A rock of several tons (generally of granite), is used for the anchor, and is taken to some place in the river which "does not interfere with navigation," and sunk. Two holes have been drilled in it and in them are secured an iron bale to which is attached a seven or eight foot chain. On the other end of the chain is a spar, (a thirty foot buoy), into the free end of which is fastened an iron clevis, like the piece of iron on the end of a cart tongue.

Four twenty-five foot poles form the square frame. The upper one or "top pole" is of spruce: the three lower ones are of hardwood. From each of the four corners of the frame radiate a forty foot guy rope, the free ends of which are fastened together.

When, in the fall, this frame is taken on the long, flat-bottomed scow to the middle of the river, the knotted end of the guy rope is attached to the iron clevis of the buoy. The tide swings the scow upriver and the frame is tipped off into the water. If the weight of the wood will not sink the frame, it is sometimes made heavier by lashing weights to the four corners, for it must stand upright across the river like a door frame. Its "top-pole" must be under water, at least, the difference of the tide's flow and ebb, which is about twelve feet here. This frame remains in the water till spring, when it is taken out, sold, destroyed, or repaired to be used next year.

With the frame, the bag net is used. One edge of it is fastened to the top of the frame. The opposite edge is held parallel to it till needed, when, by the use of guys, two big rings, an opener and a clew line, it is let down to the bottom of the frame. The net is always set at low water just as the tide is at its first flood. When the tide sets in, it pulls the net out into a bag shape and the fish go into it through the frame.

After the frame is anchored the fisherman is ready to begin work at the opening of the season, when the cold weather comes on.

Let's go out with them for a catch in the old days, in the days when there were four "strings" of boats, as the men called the different groups. In daytime the flowing ice was dotted with black scows, a muffled figure at each end: and by night their lanterns threw uncertain lights across irregular cakes of creaking ice. There was the "steam mill string," the one at Treat's wharf, and the little one at Hardy's Point called in fun, the "Mushrats:" but we will follow the middle string, of forty or fifty fishers, among them some "fellers" from the Cove.

The boats are rowed from shore till each man finds his watch buoys, one of which ought to float from each upper clew line of his net. When found, the man at each end of the boat seizes it and pulls in on the rope, thus swinging the scow across the river: they creep up closer to the frame, shorten the rope till over it. Then they haul hard on the rope till the frame comes up alongside of the boat and make fast.

They begin to haul: as the net comes out of water thin ice coats it and the ropes with shell ice falling from them are not easy to hold. It is a forty or fifty pound catch and both men must work fast and keep their wits about them, for if the running ice finds them fast to the frame, it is all up with them. They are now at the tide's mercy if it decides to play some trick. It may turn and run down while the frame is half over the boat and the net half in, or, the "freshet on this tide may run up, turn right around and go back again." The bravest of fishermen feels a relief when his ice-laden cargo is secured, the net has gone overboard, the frame has been pushed off and he is free. No doubt many a retired fisher can hear the voice of Uncle Joe Higgins, on a still and frosty night, call to the "middle string" to come this way or that, as their boats were making a way thro the ice to the eddy in shore.

If the nets are set in the evening at eight, the flood will call for the men to haul, in about four hours. For days, he may get nothing, or perhaps his reward be but a few pounds. Then he gets discouraged, lays off and spends his time in camp, smoking or telling stories, till some one gets a bushel. The news spreads fast among the camps and again the channel fills with boats.

Another "Penobscot man" here in our little village,

"And it may be that the Penobscot man is a better, wiser, more serious man than even his contemporaries have judged him to be."

93

XIV - Here and There in the Village

Time changes faces and brings new people to old homes, but lays his hands lightly on localities that here and there have been of sufficient importance in the lives of our fathers to receive a name.

Summer visitors and those returning to old home gatherings look in vain for the old acquaintance, but they may return to old haunts and scenes and know that these will be found unaltered.

In this good Prohibition state and in our very midst, long ago, Nature set a high hill, removed its top and dug an enormous cavity in its center, to which man gave the name, the Punch Bowl. There are different stories of the origin of this name: that on its slopes the Indians met for their war dances and in the hollow prepared their drinks; that when the British came up the river, they repaired to this hill to brew their punch: that a cloven hoof print on some rock bespoke the Evil One's presence at one time and the locality became the Devil's Punch Bowl.

All of this is interesting in view of the fact that owing to its peculiar formation, no water ever stands in its basin, altho as late as June snow has been found in the bottom of it. It is of granite formation and once an attempt was made to quarry it, but owing to the inferior quality of the stone, the enterprise was unsuccessful.

It has served as a picnic ground for the young people of the town and has been the scene of May parties in years gone by: the small boy hunted here, for partridges, squirrels, rabbits and for spruce gum.

One who had played there in boyhood recently visited the spot, but for him its glory had departed, most of the old trees having been cut down and the only live thing to welcome him was a gray squirrel. From this highest point in the village — one which is selected by surveyors as a signal station — there is a surprisingly wide-spread view: to the west, of country, farm and woodland, bordered on the horizon by the low-lying hills of Dixmont and Monroe: to the east, of the Bucksport hills, Cobb's Mountain and Alamoosick, — Blue Hill in the distance — with the river threading a blue line between: to the south, the home mountains. Treat's, Mount Waldo and Mosquito: and on a clear day the hard climb is repaid by a glimpse of Mount Katahdin to northward.

A young growth of birches and maples has matured along the inner slope of this bowl, whose tops are far below one who stands on the summit and he is filled with a desire to explore the depth. A descent reveals luxuriant foliage, beds of hay-scented ferns, and here and there the polypody and oak fern grow.

As one clambers up the steep side, a redstart or a vireo is scared from its nest and the odor of mint arises as it grows thro the rock-strewn grass of the rim.

A descent of the southern slope of the Punch Bowl brings one into an oak grove whose leaves indicate many varieties. These trees were set out by Doctor Manter who had secured them from various states. The field road on the "Manter farm" leads into a valley in the bed of which runs the brook — Lowe's brook — which has been followed to the bridge for trout always. From the river, about twenty or thirty rods up the brook are the remnants of a beaver dam built, no one knows how many years ago.

There is a tradition that at High Head on the river a fort or stockade was set by the early inhabitants as a protection against Indians and other intruders. But it is certain that in these later years the swallows chose its beetling brows as a safe place for their nests. At high tide vessels used to be hauled up on the shore under its banks for repairs: but now the dock is so filled that even a small boat must land a hundred feet or so from the foot of the hill and a high rock from which the boys used to dive and go swimming is now entirely covered and the salt grass grows over it.

The sweet grass grew in abundance on the shore just south of High Head and on a bank above were "the oaks." Under this group of trees some one has said: "the courting of the town was done for years." The big trees were friends of boys and girls: and a neighbor, when she returned home one night to find that they had been cut down, wept as at the loss of an old friend. When asked if she would ever have the one in front of her house cut down, she said: "No, indeed, not as long as I own it."

One of the favorite Sunday walks was to the foot of Church street where, from the eminence could be seen the boats as they came up river or made their landings. Fifty years ago there was an old cellar on this hill — grass-grown with a big rock in its center and around the edge young trees.

One day a heavy rain fell and filled the cellar so that just the top of the rock was visible. At the same time, it washed from the trees so many cat-

The Old Oak

erpillars that the place was "just alive with them: you never saw such a sight in your life," said an eye witness: and on that special Sunday afternoon the place was equally alive with people to witness the spectacle. Ever since that day the locality has been known as Caterpillar Hill.

Not far from this spot is the site of the original Sampson house, which burned and was later succeeded by the low yellow dwelling still called by the same name. Long before a town water system was heard of, Mr. Sampson had foreseen modem conveniences and introduced the pipe system into his house. Over in the field to the west was a spring which bubbled up in three or four places, and from this an aqueduct of hollow logs laid end to end carried the water into his house. Not long ago when repairs on the main road were made remnants of these logs were found.

Sampson's spring became a town institution and as one of its neighbors said: "watered the town for years, ever since I can remember." To and from it were worn many paths. Along one of them it was a common sight to see "Minister Hayes" with yoke across his shoulder, carrying two pails of water to his home near meeting house hill.

Its healing properties were known by the small boy with a sore leg who would come and sit at its edge on the bed of pennyroyal, and bathe the afflicted member knowing that it would be soothed.

When a circus came to town the animals were taken here to drink: it was interesting to watch the elephants. They would cautiously try the ground with one foot — when sure it was safe, would drink and drink till the spring seemed dry, clean their trunks on the side of the bank, then spout the water off, — to the great delight of children watching them.

A glance at some old Commercial House registers finds their pages decorated with ornate specimens of penmanship — birds' heads attached to scrolls or swans' wings, animals with red eyes — adorning long lists of names, each name perhaps terminating with an elaborate flourish. This was one way of advertising the shows with which the place was flooded in the 50's and 60's, for Frankfort was considered a good show town.

"The Great United States Circus and Menagerie."

It took two long pages to register the names of its performers — fifty-eight in all.

"Part of the Great Oriental Circus & Egyptian Caravan."

"The Great North American Circus and Hippodrome."

Probably there was no greater anticipation of the coming of these than was aroused by the brown paper hand bills on which young Toby Tyler aainounced to his own fellow townsmen.

"Big Circus
Doors open Putty Soon
Price 3 cents"

The present G. A. R. Hall has been in its day a social center. Originally it was a Congregationalist vestry and stood on Kaler street just below the Methodist church. A Mr. Holbrook bought it and moved the building to its present location on Commercial street and it was called Holbrook's Hall. Then it was "taken care of" by Joe Clark and became Clark's Hall. In it was held every kind of entertainment from "Comical Brown" to a Christmas tree. A voice from its green room would tell interesting things.

"The Hutchinson Family
Tribe of Asa
1865."

"Style and Phelps — Clog Dancers."

"Rope Tyer — Prof. Harry."

Even "Ten Nights in a Bar Room" has received applause due it from an enthusiastic audience within these walls.

The "Silver Gray Sheet and Pillow Case Ball" and many other dances were given there by the town's people.

The word dance suggests to old timers one person, old Jack Douglas. No anniversary, wedding, excursion or social gathering of any kind in that day was ever a success, without the characteristic music of his fiddle or fiddles; for Jack had a collection of them and liked to use the one best suited to his mood; some of them are now distributed about in the country.

This man known to us as Jack Douglas was a town character. It is said that he was born on the island of San Domingo probably about the year 1780. Various stories of his early life were abroad, but the old man was always reticent about himself. On one occasion, when asked how many brothers and sisters he had, he gave a gruff reply, "didn't stop to count 'em" and lapsed into silence. Uncle Billy Mansfield was the one man in whom he confided and this confidence was not misplaced.

When a boy he was drafted into the English army to serve for seven years — was for a time at Cape Verde Islands as a major: there he learned our language and came to this country as a stowaway, concealed in a hogshead.

Another story is that he ran away from home to be a drummer boy. Tiring of this life, he made his escape by swimming from the island: took his drum along, having concealed his violin in it. He was picked up by an American man-o'-war and in some way fell in with Captain John Shute of Prospect who brought him to this country about 1846.

He lived in the Shute family and plied his trade as a hatter: but it was not long before his musical ability became known and he was sought thro the surrounding towns, so made trips with the violin, sometimes by horseback and sometimes by boat. On one of these he was gone three or four months down by Machias or Calais and returned with a bride — a white woman.

He bought a small farm near "Poverty shore," cultivated it a little: organized a band of twenty-four reed pieces: gave violin lessons to a few young men thereabouts and still made trips thro the country. While away on one of them, his wife saw another colored man whom she liked better and ran away with him: but this did not dishearten Jack for he made three subsequent marriages, with a colored woman, a white woman, and, after he came to

Frankfort to live, with an Indian woman, Mary Oney. She was but fifteen and Jack, they said, was old enough to be her grandfather. She was from Dixmont, daughter of a full-blooded Indian who dressed in blankets and made baskets.

Jack lived in Frankfort for twelve or fifteen years on the Billy Mansfield farm out on Whig street. His copper-colored face framed in iron-gray hair and beard, his tall figure which stooped a little was a familiar sight as he went about on his old white horse. Jack had none of the characteristic features of the southern negro: tho Mary said that he "could play every kind of an instrument except a Jew's harp" and added that he couldn't "play that, his lips were too thick."

He was universally liked for he was good company: and could play best when he had embibed of the fire water, and everyone adds "he was always a gentleman."

He was taken on excursions on the old steamer Tarratine — to play for the dancing. People would come twenty or thirty miles to take him to a wedding.

At this time the dancing of Fanny Elssler was attracting attention: and tissue paper figures of the danseuse, attached to a sand glass in a way to make her dance, were the fashion. Captain Joshua Atwood had brought one from Boston: but for some reason the contrivance wouldn't work. So one of the assembled company suggested "let's have Jack to play for her." He came and at the first strains of Money Musk the lady began to dance. Only Jack could make the fiddle speak, only he could make her dance.

Jack composed music, could write it and talk at the same time, tho you never could get him to speak while playing. Howe's violin book contained some of his waltzes, and in other books were his compositions with suggestive names — Mountain Hornpipe, Douglas's Hornpipe and Hole in the Floor.

Then, too, he could make a violin. One of his which is most prized is partly of his own construction: the pegs he whittled of red-wood, the finger board was of bone and with his knife he fashioned the baseboard.

It is said that in the top is a piece of the negro's old hat and some writing: but no amount of curiosity will induce the owner to take it apart and read. He has refused a thousand dollars for the instrument, he says, tho he paid an old violin and seventy-five dollars for it and the additional promise "never to part with it except for bread."

Some say that the secret of Jack's accomplishments lay in the fact that he was a spiritualist: for he had faith in the spirits' workings and was guided by their directions.

A Mr. De Silver had bought Jack's old house at Poverty Shore and made some improvements on it. So he invited its former owner to come down and fiddle for the festivities of the house-warming. Jack had a homesick feeling and accepted the invitation, saying he was "going to the bone garden for a few days." A too prophetic remark! For he was taken ill and died there and was buried on the shore not far from his first home. His wife continued to live in this town, doing housework or helping in a few families and for years "aunt Mary Douglas" was a welcome caller at any fireside. Her last days, however, were spent at the poor farm.

Jack used to talk with his violin it is said and the old instrument still converses with him. As it lies in its case to-day, its owner hears raps on the box. Perhaps no attention is paid to them but they are not silent till the instrument is taken from its box, unwrapped from the silk cover and the bow drawn across the strings. Any tune will not satisfy it, for till Douglas's Favorite has been played it will not go back to its box content.

One of the first permanent places of refreshment for animals, aside from natural drinking places by

The Town Trough

the roadside, was the watering trough between the old Haley place and Tapley's Mills, on the way to Mouseville. As early as 1857 a tub was placed here by Mr. Ferrin Blaisdell, with the help of a nine-year-old son. They felled a tree from the grove above the spot and led the water into the tub. Mr. Blaisdell kept this in repair for years until the farm came into the hands of John Snow. "From James Haley's to the watering trough" was a Sunday drive.

For years the gypsies camped near the spot and their coming did not please the neighbors for they learned that the coming of a gypsy band meant a spell of rainy weather.

Years later a granite watering trough was set at the southern end of the town, a gift of Dr. Charles Abbott. In a glen back of it there used to be a fountain which sent its spray into a large round granite basin and flowed into the brook under the main road. There were steps to the brook and strollers here on Sunday afternoon must have a drink from the bubbling spring.

XV - First and Last

Public buildings were not a necessity among the settlers, to make them consider public affairs.

During the first days of their life here, a town house was not necessary in order to transact town business: the roadside, a woodpile, or a settler's cabin served just as well.

They did not wait for a schoolhouse before teaching their children: but the little ones gathered at a fireside, or around a living-room table, and with the instruction of a neighbor learned to read and write.

A church or minister were not needed for public worship: at some house or sometimes in a barn, the people gathered to hear the exhortations of a native preacher; and if the expected missionary were detained by wind or weather, the assembled company sang hymns, read the Scripture and dispersed to their homes.

As early as 1793, the question of education, of raising school money was being discussed: to make provision for the housing and teaching of children in the settlement. This was long before a house of worship for parents was thought of. When the first schoolhouse was built, it was used on Sunday as a meeting-house: thereafter, education and religion were discussed together and town meetings called for the consideration of both.

In January, 1794, the village fathers met at Captain Grant's to hear the report of a committee about hiring a schoolmaster: and at this meeting the district was divided into districts and the money divided among them.

"The district from John Kemptons to Adam Grant's red house hired a schoolmaster for one month. Daytime for Small children & evenings for Men & Large Boys. Six Dollars a month & we board him."

The first master was one Thomas Story, who by the 20th of February had taught his month in the upper part of the district and was ready to move on.

By March 1797, there was money enough for a building and another meeting was called.

"March 8, 1797. We met at Capt. Rich's to see what our school district should do about building a School House & we agreed to build one & agreed with James Stubbs to get the frame 22 feet by 18 for 20 Dollars it is to be 9 feet clear in the walls & all white pine except braces & studs."

It must have been built slowly as in 1800, a Mr. Thayer was keeping school at the widow Rich's.

Five years later, a schoolhouse was built near the present Sampson street, and was used the following year for town meetings. The later teachers of this school were Mr. Ricker: the late T. W. Vose of Bangor and ex-Secretary of State, Sumner Chadborne of Augusta.

On the site of the Atwood block on Main street, stood the old brick schoolhouse which was torn down in 1850, but it is still living in many minds. It was a low building; set back from the street and approached by two flights of steps. The up street and down street children went here, a little room for the little ones and a big room for the older children. Two wide aisles separated its three rows of desks and led up some steps to the platform, to the master's desk — an uphill road, the path of learning. One still lives among us who presided here and many remember her wise teaching. One master is not forgotten. In winter he had a hundred pupils and could not possibly hear all the little ones say their letters: so he heard a few, then taking a child on each knee, finished the lesson by telling them all a story.

To the children the desk looked like a pulpit. Perhaps it was meant to inspire them, and on Sabbath day it was used as one.

In this house the Congregationalists held services while the chapel farther down the street was closed. Here came Unitarian, Trinitarian, Methodists and Congregationalists to decide about building a new church, and from these plans came the church on the hill. Baptist preachers drew their followers here and roused the village to a revival and laid the foundations for a new church.

In 1833 there was a Select school. It had a first department and a second department, presided over by an instructor and an instructress. The names of its pupils were enrolled as males and females, one hundred and thirty-eight in all, of whom but eleven were living in 1901.

Many of us can remember the evening time, in our early years, when after the supper dishes were cleared and grandfather came in from the barn, he put on his specs, took the big Bible from its place on the shelf near the clock, and sat at the end of the table, which stood against the wall after its leaves had been turned down. He began to read the Word, and expected the children to pay attention. But if the childish mind wandered, a quick call of the delinquent's name, made her turn and meet the eyes of her elder, peer over the steel bows — "Listen now!" No church was needed for that service and the days held more time for worship and discussion of the soul's affairs than they do now. The fact that such attempts were made is shown by to-day's old family Bibles and the Bible is all that is left of some of these families to-day.

So, a hundred years ago, each house was a fit place for service, and each took its turn as a meeting-house.

"Anthony preached at Bolan's."

"Mr. Hall preached at Josiah Colson's."

"Mr. Anthony preached at Whittam's."

"Sunday Meeting at Mr. Oakman's New House."

"Mr. Wager preached at Littlefield's. Wife went."

"In a snowstorm went to Mrs. Rich's to hear Mr. Mudge preach but he did not come. They sang songs & we came home.

"A new Methodist preacher at Mr. Bolan's to day, his name is Tim Merritt from Conn."

Preachers well known in early church history worked here and sought the souls of men. Jesse Lee, Joshua Hall and the Reverend Enoch Mudge of the Methodist faith; Paul Coffin and Parson Sewell, the Congregationalist; and the Baptist elder, Simon Emery. Then there were the Jesuit missionaries, Chiampi, Virgillinto, Vetromele and Father Bapst.

The Methodists began their teachings here when in 1793, Jesse Lee left his followers in Massachusetts, Boston and vicinity to undertake the conversion of what is now the whole state of Maine. Stories of his endeavors are to-day rehearsed, of the building of the first Maine meeting-house, of his travels and of how he swam his horse across the Penobscot in order to meet an appointment at Hampden.

When his work called him elsewhere, brother Joshua Hall came to Maine and in 1795 formed what was called the Penobscot circuit. This comprised the towns east and west of the Penobscot river. He also joined the towns of Hampden, Orrington and Frankfort into a society and it is said that in spite of hardships and violent opposition his efforts were successful.

The Reverend Enoch Mudge came next, settled at Orrington, from which place he fulfilled his pastoral duties along the river. The life of the missionary preacher in those days was full: long journeys were his, entertained in comfortless dwellings and often partaking of hard fare. This divine, shortly after he settled, took to himself a wife and his publishment certifies

"That the Rev. Enoch Mudge formerly of Lynn but now a resident of Orrington and the Widow Jerusha Hinkley of Orrington hath been lawfully Published & that their Intention of Marriage hath been entered fourteen Days prior to the Date of this Certificate. Solomon Swett Town Clerk, Orrington, Oct. 27, 1797."

The marriage ceremony was performed by Doctor Goodwin, who happily comments upon the event and its effect on the divine.

"Oct. 29, 1797. Went up to Orrington Meeting House with my wife in Capt. Rich's Boat & there married the Rev. Enoch Mudge to the Widow Jerusha Hinkley in the Said Meeting House. A Parson Merritt preached in the forenoon & in the afternoon, Mr. Mudge, a very fine sermon. I think he preached the better for being married — be that as it may it was the best sermon I ever heard him preach."

The Methodist Society grew in these parts and finally Frankfort became the strongest church in the circuit; the boundaries of these districts had changed from time to time.

So, with other denominations in the village, the members began to consider the question of building a church. There had been chapels. After deliberation it was built, what is now the Congregationalist Church and was known as the Union Meeting-house. The building was dedicated In January 1832, and its pulpit was to be occupied by ministers of the different denominations which had built it and in time proportioned according to their contributions. After a while, however, differences arose amongst them and the Methodists sold out to the Congregationalists and held meetings in the present Congregationalist vestry, until in 1850 when they built the church which they now occupy.

There is a long list of the good men who have ministered here: among those of later years are Elder E. H. Small, Reverend T. B. Tapper, Mr. Bolton, Mr. Springer, Mr. Jewell, and George Pratt. Associated closely with the church work are the citizens. Job Lord, Reuben Rich, Chandler Goodwin and many others.

The church building has been little changed in exterior, but some repairs have been made inside. The pulpit used to be in the west end of the house and thus all seats faced the door, with the singer's seats in the rear.

One who was in the congregation at the dedicatory service remembers that the sermon was on church manners. The listeners were to notice strangers and give them prompt attention and welcome: to walk into church on the balls of the feet, thus disturbing no one: and the men were reminded to remove their hats on entering the vestibule and not put them on till that point was reached again. The Congregationalist Church, the first one to be erected in town, is now the finest location on the river; and its spire first bids us welcome as the river bears us home. As we know its early history is that of the Methodist society.

The lot chosen for its foundation, at that first business meeting in the old schoolhouse, was on the hill between the Washburn land and that of Esquire Jones. This was originally a part of a ten-acre lot sold off from the Ephraim Grant farm. This ledge, as it was designated, was determined upon and the future church was to be modeled after the (then) New Orrington meetinghouse at a cost of $3000.

Calvin Rider was the contractor and his work stands good to-day, strong and well built. The uneven sides of its heavy beams show hand work and are held together by heavy wooden pins. Its general lines remain the same, but repairs from time to time have greatly altered the interior.

The dedicatory service was held in 1834. An attendant at church on that day on entering by either door, found himself in a large vestibule. He exchanged good morning with his neighbors, and while he waited for the crowd to pass in, his eye rested on a little square box, fastened to the wall near one of the doors which led up the short flight of steps to the gallery. This was the publishment box and its little glass front was of interest to churchgoers and contained more mystery than did the old way of crying the marriage intentions in the street.

As he passed under the gallery into the church, past the box-stove in either corner, he was shown a seat half way up the aisle and the pew door was closed. While waiting for service to begin, the eye wandered to the arch over the high pulpit which bore the inscription

"Dedicated to the Service of Almighty God, in the Year of Our Lord 1833."

Many a little girl has studied that or admired the crimson hangings and their tassels, which draped the pulpit, while wishing for the service to be over.

The service was much the same as now, except that the congregation stood during the prayer and faced the choir, while the hymns were sung. The gallery extended across the width of the house and along it was a railing over which hung red baize curtains. When service began, they were pushed back, and he saw the singers: one of the Kempton girls and Mary Haley's mother. Even now, some new bonnet, lace kerchief, silken shawl, black silk mits or dainty fan, worn on that day is remembered. Then there was Laura Little, and Mrs. Powers, and on either side Ben Cushing played the bass viol and Sewell Tapley, the violin. All were led by Mr. Cobb, the singing-school master.

The sermon was preached by Reverend E. Frothingham, a Unitarian minister from Belfast.

There was living at Roxbury, Massachusetts, at this time, a man who is described as "another example of the success which is almost certain to result from industry and thrift." This was Benjamin Bussy, who had been in the Revolution, had later acquired a fortune by engaging in foreign commerce and who used it to generous ends. Mrs. Benjamin Shaw, a member of the union society, interested him in it and he presented a bell — a "Paul Revere bell." The same Paul Revere who is a hero in history was also a silversmith, a bell founder, and from his own shop grew works which still retain his name — the Revere works. The boy who climbs to the top of our belfry will find in heavy letters across the bell, "Revere, Boston."

Our bell was accepted with due ceremony and it was voted that it be rung at half past seven in the morning, twelve at noon, nine in the eve until the twentieth of March and also that it be rung on the Sabbath for meetings as is usual in other places: and when Mr. Bussy went up the river on some trip it was rung in his honor.

The Sunday-school children presented the Bible in 1858.

Many repairs were made in 1860, the roof slated, part of the gallery removed, pulpit lowered and the doors taken from the pews. In October of the same year, the clock was purchased by subscription and put up.

The Congregationalist Society was organized in the town in 1820 and consisted of three male members. Deacon Thomas Colbum, Mr. Richard Thurston and Bailey Peirce. Preaching was supplied by the missionary society. Four years later, the society, now increased to eight members, had an ordained minister, Mr. Jubilee Wellman. Its services were held in the schoolhouse, then in a chapel which stood on land now the head of Kaler street. Then came the union of churches, the severing of this union, after which the first resident preacher of the new society was the Reverend S. S. Tappan, who built the Cushing homestead and occupied it. Among other pastors have been, S. N. Hayes. Mr. Wright and Mr. Blanchard.

From the brick schoolhouse meetings was started another church, this time the Baptist. A Mr. Charles G. Porter came to the village and held revival meetings thro the fall and winter, with such success that there were enough converts to think of building a meeting-house. A plot of land was bought near the head of Church street in 1843 and a small building erected. Names associated with this church were the Roweels, the Kelleys, Couilliards, Fernalds and Tapleys.

A citizen in town says that they must have had a good Sunday-school for he remembers many a Sunday morning of being called at four to get his lesson.

For years after Mr. Sargent went away the building was not used and was finally torn down in 1882.

About the year '47 when the lumber mills were flourishing and the shipyards needed hands, a few Irishmen came to the village seeking employment.

They either brought families or married here and there grew to be quite a settlement in the southern end of the town. Of course they soon felt the need of a place of worship. For some time they met at private houses; the McDermott, McDonaugh, Goodnow or Haley homes, and were ministered to by the missionaries whom the Catholic Church had sent thro the Maine territory.

In many parts of the country there was bitter feeling against their faith, and its followers suffered many hardships at the hands of some narrow-minded Protestants. The same feeling crept into the village of Frankfort and many times mass was said in secret: when the church was finally built, it had to be guarded at night. Those were the times that "tried men's souls."

One of the secret meeting-places, was the barn now attached to the Wharf house: this was originally the Haley house and stood on the site of the Abbott watering trough, and was a haven for worshipers. Often here was entertained the Swiss missionary, Father Bapst: here too he came for refuge after his unhappy experience at Ellsworth.

As only two or three men were assigned to this large territory, remote towns were visited by a priest once or possibly twice a year: among those who came were Fathers O'Sullivan and Moor: and the Jesuit priests, Bapst, Dunacre, Chiampi, Virgillinto, Eugene Vetromele and Michael Gallagher.

The lot for the Catholic Church building was purchased from Mr. Sproul in 1851 and the church erected in 1853. It was Father Bapst, who at that time was residing at Oldtown and had this place, with Ellsworth, Cherryfield and Bucksport as his mission, who was instrumental in building the church: he also presented it with the copy of Raphael's masterpiece which till a few years ago hung over the altar.

The first resident priest was the Reverend Father Jeremiah McCarthy now of Houlton, Maine. Others were Fathers Duddy and Coffy and to-day the Reverend Father P. J. Garrity ministers to the parish which includes Winterport, Frankfort and Bucksport.

The Reverend Father John Bapst was born in LaRoche, a village of the canton of Fribourg, Switzerland, December 1815. He studied at the college of Fribourg, entered the novitiate of Superior Jesuits in 1835. He was ordained a priest in 1848, and two years later came to America where he was assigned all the missions of Maine and resided at Eastport on the border.

From 1848 to 1851, at the request of the Bishop of Boston, he was placed in charge of the Indian mission at Oldtown and was assisted for a time by Father Chiampi. Some of the old squaws still remember him: one, of how "he married me" or "use try teach us leetle English." There has been no resident priest on the Island since he left, altho it was under the care of the Jesuits till '55.

In 1853 Father Bapst moved to Bangor and was placed in charge of the eastern missions, living there till '59. His work took him to Machias, to Waterville and to the river towns. It was at this time that he met with the treatment at Ellsworth which nearly cost him his life.

One dark, cold and dismal night, he was seized by a mob of fanatics, robbed of his watch, dragged to a shipyard, tarred, feathered and left in this wretched condition. He recovered enough to crawl to a house nearby, was taken in by the owner, a Protestant, and cared for by him: when the mob came again he was ready to defend the priest at the cost of his own life.

It was on his way back to Bangor that Father Bapst sought refuge with the Haley family: and on his return to the city, the merchants and citizens called an indignation meeting at City Hall, denouncing the outrage.

For a long time the owners of vessels hailing from Ellsworth changed the hailing name, so that they would not be known in other parts. When in 1862, he went to Boston to become Rector of Boston College, and later pastor of the Church of the Immaculate Conception, he was hailed as the "gentle Swiss missionary who had suffered the outrages in Maine" and whom "cultivated Boston, feeling shame for its northern kindred, received kindly and his character soon won him the friendship of eminent citizens."

He died in Baltimore in 1887 and a brother priest who knew him personally in his later years, says he was loved by all who knew him and who came in contact with him.

A tribute to him in the younger years of his work is no less beautiful, that "he was beloved by all people, not only of his own flock, but by those of all denominations."

He is spoken of tenderly by the little girl for whom he would wash dishes if she cut his day's allowance of tobacco, and after the work was done, as a surprise a lump of maple sugar from his pocket, was slipped into her hand.

He is spoken of tenderly by the old man, who on a terribly cold night, the last of the old year, went to Bangor to ask him to drive thirteen miles and minister the last rites to the dying. He never refused to relieve suffering. Yet, forgetful of self, on that night of his cruel treatment at Ellsworth, he could not be persuaded to take nourishment, lest he break the fast prescribed to be observed between midnight and the hour for celebrating mass.

Aided by his parishioners in Bangor, he had erected a large church, of which one of them said: "When you go to Bangor next time, and see the spire of St. John's Catholic Church pointing heavenward, think kindly of him." This is his monument.

The well-known churchyard of other New England towns is not to be found in old Frankfort. As the church was the last public building to be put up, how could there be a churchyard? Homes were remote and each family generally laid its own to rest in a corner of the field or wood lot. Today slate stones stand or lie on farms and are hard to find unless some one knows the way. They are scattered; the burial place of Jane Prince Goodwin; the few stones of the Kemptons at Oak Point; the Ide burying-ground in the field at New Frankfort; the Grant lot out by the stream: this seemed a common custom.

At the Cove, on the hillside, lie two little ones, the children of Mr. Sullivan. They had died of scarlet fever and he came up from Castine on a furlough, put the little ones in a rough box and buried them on his farm, the first cemetery in town.

There was no general burial place till John Oakman gave to the town a half acre of land, which was to be fenced in. This was on Oakman hill and to that part of the cemetery have been added new lots: old fences with their inscriptions, or gates bearing daguerreotypes have disappeared: old trees, iron and chain fences and the time-silvered picket fences have dropped apart. Now the beautiful spot takes in Oak Hill and Memorial Park. There stands a high granite shaft, as much a monument to him whose thought and generosity presented it to the town, as to the brave men who went from the town to the front in '61.

It was the gift of the Honorable Theophilus Cushing and its dedication in September, 1871, will long be remembered. From far and near the people came and a thousand were fed on the hill that day.

The speaker of the day was Colonel Thomas Wentworth Higginson, who gave an eloquent and thrilling address. At the close of his oration Mr. Cushing made the presentation speech and the gift was feelingly accepted for the town by Elisha Arey, first selectman. Mr. Higginson told the donor that he had never seen so much bunting in all his life. It was draped from one end of town to the other.

The bronze tablets on the sides of the monument bear fitting sentiments and the names of the men who went to war from the town.

A volume might be written about the men from this town who served their country: about this or that company; about the men who were at Little Round Top, at Shiloh or Gettysburg; about those who suffered in rebel prisons; of him who to-day wears a medal of honor for his bravery, the little man who captured the rebel flag from its height; of women who sewed and picked lint and packed boxes; of the young ladies who knit socks and sent them to the boys. They are the story of every community.

The town books show how Lincoln's repeated calls for Volunteers were received and it is a pity that the vote cast soon after the war to preserve careful records of our part in it was not carried out.

But the spirit of the men and their resolutions still live — "We desire to ignore all minor differences and divisions of the past and rally round our common country."

THE END.

Appendices

Vessels Built at Frankfort and the Marsh

Name.	Kind.	Tons.	Draught.	When.	Where.	By Whom.	Remarks.
Ada S. Wiswell....	Sch.	198	9	'54	Marsh ...		
Addison Gilbert...	Ship	861	20	'55	Frankfort.	Dunhams	In '81 hailed as Uno from Norway.
Albert Treat......	Sch.	149	10	'59	Marsh....		To West Indies and Prince Edward's Island.
Alice.............	"	99	10	'59	Frankfort.	Treat & Co......	
Annie Bell	"	213	11	60 or 61	Marsh....		Built for Captain Crocker, P. E. I. Trader.
Ansdell	Bk.	328	12	'54	"		* F. S. Means.
Ann Eliza.........	Sch	97	9	'70	"	F. Treat & Co...	Mackerel fisher to Bay of Chaleur.
Anna..............		601		'59	Frankfort.	Treat & Co.....	* Czarina.
Augusta	Bark	422	12	'63	"		'81 hailed from Sweden. * Mary A. Rich.
Alpine	"						Bone and Muscle.
Annie M. Rich....	Sch.				F........	Dunham........	Built for Wheeler Hardy.
Arabella..........	Bq.				"	"	
Arey....	Ship	1207	21	'56	"	Williams & Arey.	Later called Caroline ; then Nautilus, last.
Albus.............						Dunham........	
Adams Treat......					Marsh....		
Argus					"		
Eddie P. Treat....	Sch.				Marsh		
Franklin....	"	92		1810	Frankfort.		
Flor del Mer......	Bk.	625	14	'63	Marsh....		In Spanish, Flower of the sea. Later named Kate Merrill, then Kate.
Fannie	Bq.	155		'53	Frankfort.	Williams........	
France	Ship	363	18	'56	"	Dunham........	
Frank Treat	Sch.				Marsh....		
Forest Bell.......		84		'69	Frankfort.		Rebuilt at Winterport '69. Then 22 years old .
Frank Treat					"	Williams........	
Gibraltar....... ..	Ship	721	19	'54	"		
George Treat......	Bk.	639		'66	"		
Gipsey		33	6	'68	Winterp't.	J. & C. H. Treat.	* Polly Ann.
Hesperus	Sch.	88	8	'64			
Harriet Churchill..					F...	Treat & Co......	
Hattie Hilliard....	Sch.				Marsh....		
Isabella Jewett....	"	173		'53	Frankfort.		Alive '84.
James M. Churchill	Bk.				F..... ...	Treat & Co.. ...	
John Dwyer.......				'64	"	"	
John Henry.......	Bk.				"		
Joan	Bq.				Marsh....		
L. J. Knight......	Sch.	203		'53	"		
L. W. Rich..							
Lucy M. Collins...		167		'67	F........	Dunham & Eveleth	
Lucinda Maria....					"	Williams........	
Lath. Rich.......	Sch.	190		'55	"	Dunhams	
Light Boat........	"	121	9	'61	Marsh....		
Libertad..........		526	15	'64	"		Liber'y in Spanish.

108

Name.	Kind.	Tons.	Draught.	When.	Where.	By Whom.	Remarks.
Mexican	Sch.	92		'72			Rebuilt. Coaster.
Mary B. Rich	Bk.			'56?			
Mariel	Sch.	84	9	'51			
M. A. Herrera	Bq.	385	15	'58	F.	Treat & Co.	
Mary E. Long							
Maria Hopkins							Lost first trip.
Marion A. Gords.	Sch.				Marsh		
Nancy & Hannah	Bq.			before 1829	F.		
" Treat	Bk.			'48	Marsh		
Nonpareil		1097	21	'54	F.		
Orion				1807	F.	Andrews, Ware & Dean.	
Robert Treat	Ship.				Marsh.		Largest vessel built at
Reynard					F.	Dunham.	Marsh.
Rippling Waves		180	9	'66	Marsh.		
Ruth Thomas		97	10	'45	"		
Robert Byron		96	11	'70	"		Alive '84.
Restless		259	11	'62	Oct.		* E. P. Treat.
Robin	Bq.	309	12	'57	Frankfort		
Robert E. Woodruff					"	J. & Ch. Treat.	Rebuilt at Winterport.
Speedwell	Sch.			'74			
"	"	691	19	'54-'72	F.	Dunhams	
Spitfire	Sch.	1520	21	'53	F.	"	Capt. Crocker says 1505 T.
Sadie Corey		156		'80	Winterp'rt		*Lucy Church. Reb'lt here.
Savannah	"	67		'70	Marsh.		
Sparkling Sea		278	13	'58	"		
Samuel Larrabee					F.	Treat & Co.	
Sarah Parker	Bq.				Marsh		
T. K. Weldon		405	15	'65	Marsh.	Doyle & White	
J. O. Thompson	Bk.	130	10	'46	Frankfort.	Williams.	
T. O. Cunningham.	Bq.				"	"	
Warren	Bk.				Marsh.		Built on same block as Libertad—Flor del Mer.
William				Before '29	Frankfort.		
Wings of the Wind	Ship	944	21	'52	"	Dunham	* Flying Arrow.
Wild Pigeon							
William	Sch.	89		'39			
Webster	Bq.				Marsh.		

Sources of Information

Abbott Diary, 1805.

Abbott's History of Maine.

Acadia, Whipple.

Account of the Rise and Fall of Methodism in Hamden Circuit.

American Lloyd's Shipping Register, 1867-'76.

" Navigation, W, W. Bates.

Ancient Dominions of Maine, 1859, R. K. Sewall.

Avery Genealogy.

Bancroft's History of the United States.

Bangor Historical Magazine.

Brewer's Journal of Penobscot Indians.

Bucksport Town Records.

Chadwick Survey Chart.

China Collectors in America, Alice Morse Earle.

Commercial House Registers.

Commissioner's Report of Maine.

Coolidge and Mansfield's History of Maine, 1860.

Court Records of Boston, 1699-1723, 1746-49, 53-55, 57-76.

Description of New England Towns, 1859, Coolidge and Mansfield.

Diary of Francis Le Baron Goodwin.

" Seth Noble, Bangor.

Dictionary of American Biography, Drake.

Discovery of the Penobscot River, Archibald Jones.

Drake's Book of Indians, 1833.

Davis, Honorable William, Plymouth.

Furniture of the Olden Time, Frances Clary Morse.

Genealogical Register, 1853.

Geographical Names of Coast Survey, C. S. Report, 1868, Rev. Edward Ballard.

Hancock County Deeds

Harlan and Hollingsworth, Wilmington, Delaware.

Herrick's Field Note Book, 1808.

History of Belfast, Williamson.

History of Castine, Penobscot and Brooksville, George Augustus Wheeler.

" Catholic Church in the New England States.

" Frankfort, MSS.. Archibald Jones.

" Maine, Williamson.

" Massachusetts, Hutchinson.

" Merchant Shipping, 1816-1874, W. S. Lindsay.

" Methodism in Maine, 1887, Chas. E. Nash.

" the Mission of the United Brethren Among the Indians in New England, 1794.

Historical Register of Officers of the Revolution, Heitman.

" Sketch of Frankfort, E. Parker Treat.

Homes of Family Names, H. B. Guppy.

Home Life in Colonial Days, Alice Morse Earle.

Letters of Francis Le Baron Goodwin.

" Kempton Family.

Life of Col. Paul Revere, Goss.

" Count Rumford, George D. Ellis.

Lincoln County Deeds.

List of Merchant Vessels for the United States

Lloyd's Shipping Register

Map of the Town of Frankfort, 1855, D. S. Osborn.

Memoirs of Champlain, 1804.

Monroe Town Record.

Newspapers

Bangor Register, 1819,

Christian Herald, 1845.

Frankfort Gazette, 1855.

Volunteer, 1863.

Waldo Gazette, 1839.

Official Record of Union and Confederate Navies in the War of the Rebellion, 1862.

Old Account Books

" Deeds.

" Paths and Legends of New England, Katharine Abbott.

Old Tombstones at Frankfort

" Oak Hill Cemetery.

" Private Yards.

" Plymouth.

Prospect Town Records

" Publishments.

" Weather Report.

Probate Records of Lincoln County, 1760-1800.

Peter's Field Notes — First Survey of Penobscot River,

Record of Congregational Church.

Report of Earl Tax Collectors.

Revised Statutes of Maine.

Shipmasters' Association Report.

Soldiers of the American Revolution, C. J. House.

Some Colonial Homesteads, Marion Harlan.

Sullivan's History of the District of Maine, 1795.

Travels in New England, President Dwight of Yale.

True Story of Paul Revere, Chas. Ferris Guttemy.

Two Centuries of Costume in America, Alice Morse Earle.

Varney's Gazetteer, 1886.

Waymouth Tercentenary, Maine Historical Society.

Winterport Town Record.